For Gordon & Dorothy

from Michael Burn

Wales November 2008

Poems as Accompaniment to a Life

Also by Michael Burn

FULL THROTTLE
(for Sir Henry Birkin)

WHEELS TAKE WINGS
(a history of Brooklands)

ALAN PARSONS' SCRAPBOOK
(an anthology, with Viola Tree)

THE LABYRINTH OF EUROPE

MR LYWARD'S ANSWER

THE DEBATABLE LAND

THE AGE OF SLATE

MARY AND RICHARD

TURNED TOWARDS THE SUN

Fiction

YES, FAREWELL

CHILDHOOD AT ORIOL

THE MIDNIGHT DIARY

THE TROUBLE WITH JAKE

Poetry

POEMS TO MARY

THE FLYING CASTLE

OUT ON A LIMB

OPEN DAY AND NIGHT

KEATS POETRY PRIZE, 1973

Play

THE MODERN EVERYMAN

Poems as Accompaniment to a Life

MICHAEL BURN

MICHAEL RUSSELL

First published in Great Britain
by Michael Russell (Publishing) Ltd
Wilby Hall, Wilby, Norwich NR16 2JP

Page makeup in Sabon
by Waveney Typesetters, Wymondham, Norfolk
Printed and bound in Great Britain
by Biddles Ltd, King's Lynn, Norfolk

ISBN 978-0-85955-300-1

FOR JONATHAN IN MEMORY OF MARY

Taking my torch, making sure of candles,
I am come to my neighbour's home,
Old comrade, one of the last,
Not knowing clearly why I have come,
Unless to know some reason for the warning
Of urgent power-cuts,
That open memories of our old scars;
And why what once prevailed no more prevails,
The shared hopes, common cause,
That dove-wind in our sails,
The cliffs appearing,
And on the quays the girls and soldiers cheering
Freedom, and Love, and ours the last of wars;
The ship's leap forward and the shouts of joy
For Ithaca! A new-born Ithaca!
A happy Ithaca! And never back to Troy!

This is our death that haunts and never dies,
Under cold moons and internecine stars.

He has no answer.
We talk of her instead,
He being the last who knew her. I take my torch,
Walk home, and light two candles,
As she and I once used to do, in Wales,
Married, when power-cuts hardly mattered,
But cannot write.
Just sit, remembering.

You came to my candles pale in an hour of heartache,
When the angel-coat you had worn had been torn from
  your shoulders,
Young, a protester,
With only a guitar.
I told you of her.
You took what I told you of her upon the strings
Of your guitar, of your heart.
I am young again, I write.

Go, lyttel Booke. I offer it to you,
Who are like my fallen comrades,
Who might have been her child.

Contents

GROUP THREE

GROUP FOUR

GROUP FIVE

GROUP SIX

GROUP SEVEN

GROUP EIGHT

Preface

Poetry has a power to convey in a few lines, even a single line, something that in prose may run to pages. In the summer of 2003 Michael Russell published an autobiography of mine called *Turned Towards the Sun.* I supposed I had nothing more to say in prose and could get on with or back to poetry. It dismayed me, re-reading the book, to become aware that a question, implicit throughout, and never far from my mind while writing it, had nowhere been put point-blank and certainly not answered. I had been born with more privileges than millions even dream of and ever since had more than my share of health and luck. Offered so many opportunities, what had I learnt and done with them?

The question turned especially upon two longings. One began as a mission to save the world, inspired at the time of my confirmation in Winchester College Chapel when I was sixteen. For several months I was resolved to give my life to God. Later, shocked into awakening by my first glimpse of unemployment in Britain during the middle 1930s, my mission became more modest and more practical and turned into a resolve to strike some blow against social injustice. Reviewers of my book duly noted that, desperate for a panacea, I had been drawn first, for a brief while, to German National Socialism (though never to British or any other form of Fascism); then to Communism (though never to the Communist Party); and also to what I called my third autocracy, the Roman Catholic Church. Many of the socially conscience-stricken turned towards one or the other of this triad at the time, several converting between two; but no one I know of towards all three.

My tolerant, athlete, Anglican, Tory father thought of them all as a 'phase', was more worried about my refusal to take up membership of the MCC, for which he had put me down at birth, and assumed that I would 'get through' them; as I did, retaining honour for aspects of the last two. In writing about my book, A. N. Wilson correctly placed me as belonging positively to an ideological age, now (it seems to me) in many regions superseded by negative distrust and mockery for almost everything political. Yet I realised that in my book I offered hardly a clue to what, politically and religiously, I believe now.

My other longing was for requited love. Requited it was, for two years as lovers and twenty-eight in marriage, until her death, with a woman, Mary, described by Michael Russell in the book's blurb, using an eloquent restraint unusual in a blurb (though not for him), as 'remarkable by any standard'. Our marriage too was unusual. A second, principal thing I learnt from my book was that I had written too much about myself there, and too little about her.

It became a joy, as I began to select and/or complete these poems, to realise that I could use them to reduce those chasms in my autobiography. I scarcely needed to alter a single line, and none of importance, or write any new ones with that aim. After necessary compressions and eliminations that are a characteristic of poetry, the material had all been at hand. It would call for notes, and some kind of essay as a preface. I had misgivings, initially, about both. Poems should stand on their own merits. Notes would look too like crutches, and a preface like a wheelchair, to help them into acceptance by readers they had meagre hope of reaching unaided; let alone into posterity.

But notes there had to be, for explanation. After many months of indecision about the poems' presentation that ever-blessed moment arrived, the work seemed to decide for itself the shape and structure it preferred. It would be narrative, only roughly chronological, essentially moving according to development of those two longings, or 'aspirations' There are now eight groups, divided into two parts, with notes, the first five groups being on the whole more lighthearted than the last three, apart from the poems about the war and Colditz in Group One.

I cannot think of myself as a professional poet like those men and women I admire and envy, who have devoted most of their lives to the study and practice of poetry, in which I include its criticism and (so exacting and so fruitful) its translation. I have been too much the journalist, too easily distracted. The poems in this book hitherto unpublished (slightly fewer than half) emerged from heaps of folders, loose sheets, backs of envelopes and scribbles inside the hard covers of my own and other people's books, hoarded over decades. Sheaves have gone into the bin. Some have appeared suddenly, like illegitimate children demanding recognition, mostly from the last twenty years; a few are *juvenilia,* grandchildren from as long as sixty years ago; one, in one of the last groups, is a mature infant born of the war in Iraq. All have been a challenge, and remained in my head as companions, in dark hours especially; hence one reason for the title of this book. In it I have used the word 'accompaniment', in part because of its association with music; imagining a concerto with the poems as the single instrument asking for attention, and the autobiography the orchestra in the background, for which, when I have to refer to it, I use some such phrase as 'I have described elsewhere'.

I asked several friends what they thought of the idea of publishing poetry with notes to explain them. All were in favour. Four said that they didn't read much poetry, because they found it 'impenetrable' This pleased me, because I do not think it true of mine. None of my friends was over forty, three in their teens. The shock came when, from other comments of theirs, it dawned on me that my own largely classical-humanist, Christian-Scriptural education is now a bit old-hat. They had never heard of some of the folk in these poems, real or mythical, whom I took for granted. A boy of seventeen, for example, did not know who Pontius Pilate was. One of my own family pronounced Eurydice (the title of a poem in memory of Mary) 'Yury-dicey'. I have therefore added some short notes to put this deficiency right, and can now go on to a few details about myself.

To begin chronologically: I was born on 11 December 1912, twenty months before the outbreak of World War One. In 1928, at school at Winchester, I was awarded the King's Gold Medal for English Verse for lines on the compulsory subject of Stonehenge.

Best erased without trace, but unfortunately published in the school magazine, they showed the kind of promise that must have caused any critic in his right mind to assume that I was unlikely to be invited into print again; not, anyhow, in verse. (Nor was I, for the next seventeen years.) New College, Oxford, awarded me, on a history paper, an open classical scholarship. I left however (of my own free will) after a year, to write two books about motor racing and help to edit a literary anthology. Eighteen months of provincial journalism in Gloucestershire followed before I joined *The Times*, where during 1937–39 I had the impressive title of assistant to the Imperial and Foreign News Editor, Mr Deakin. World War Two came next. Having already been commissioned in a Territorial battalion of the King's Royal Rifle Corps, I was called up; but left it to volunteer for a body of risk-seeking enthusiasts called the Independent Companies, supposed to become guerrilla fighters holding up the triumphant advance of the German armies into Norway. We spent the spring and early summer of 1940 running away from them. Back home unscathed, I volunteered for the newly formed Commandos; was captured, on the night of 28/29 March 1942, during the joint Commando/Royal Navy assault on St Nazaire; and spent the last two and a half years of the war in the castle of Colditz.

Many dear friends of mine were killed at St Nazaire. My own life changed that night too. In Group One, which now follows, the last four words of Poem 1, which has them for its title, express that change. Poems 2 to 5 relate to events before the war, but were written after it. All the rest in Group One, except Poem 7, date from Colditz.

GROUP ONE

I

War Cut the String

I had a pudding face and two round eyes,
A nose beneath them, lower down a mouth.
I had fair hair, won almost every prize,
And stole, but did not need the things I stole.

At fifteen and sixteen was not unhappy,
Told fascinating lies. Mother would die,
I said, if I was beaten for a theft.
Later I grew more settled in the lie.

The dunes were warm and silk. Naked I loved them.
A mile along, someone had sketched a *plage,*
Parents like dwarfs, and running dots of friends.
I liked them thus. Close, they became too large.

I wanted to have friends among the poor.
I know I loved. Sometimes, reason unknown,
I hurried out at night and lay face down
On floors of chapels or the forest floor.

I tried to stab another boy. Forgiven,
I came of age, travelled, was promising,
Was bought pinstripes, became a charming puppet,
And learnt the dance. Enough. War cut the string.

For my friends the string had been cut with life, with all life. For me, the poem describes a loosening of links with part of the life I had led before the war: prizes at school, the beach at Le Touquet made fashionable by my grandfather, with that adumbration of disconnection from my own family and society.

2

In Memory of Viola Tree

1938

No neat equations in her life,
No endings elegantly tied
Extravagance rather, overflowings,
Friend, lover, mother, mistress, wife,

Whose blithe exuberance, exempt
From laws of waste, kept five or six
In youth and health, outdoors or in,
Tenants of her bulging tent.

All Bohemia has not seen
Such a flinging down of brilliant
Cards on patchwork quilts, of language
Such a hyperbolic queen.

If she saw a seagull swoop,
'Look, the albatross!' she'd cry.
Not odd to her to hunt flamingo
And use them as a croquet hoop.

She turned a barn into a home,
But might have married with a duke,
And said she should have been a pirate,
And in the teapot found a mouse,

And served up vaudeville with ham,
Where spiders made one look up Shakespeare
And flies hummed *lieder*, and a wasp
Was Byron stomping through the jam.

She made a swamp enchanted ground.
She jug-terued the nightingales,
And what she did for money will
Be known when Homer's grave is found.

Except a column in the Press.
I wonder how many survive
Of those her weathercock pen advised.
Do they at times wear fancy dress,

And dare to dwell in pleasure-domes,
Half-dormitory and half-stage,
And give asylum to young blades,
Self-exiled from more prudent homes?

I loved the unadmonishing,
The uncensorious careless care,
The never cold, the sometimes sad,
The seldom unastonishing,

Who most of all astonished me
By ceasing suddenly to laugh,
And then to smile. I had not thought
Her capable of inconstancy.

It's long since she was out of breath.
I shiver by that door again,
Speechless, aghast, incredulous...
My first experience of death.

This was my discovery of the vie de Bohème. *With Viola (daughter of the flamboyant actor-manager-showman Sir Herbert Beerbohm Tree, and widow of Alan Parsons) and her children David and Virginia I felt at home and prolonged my adolescence.*

3
Abdication

DECEMBER 1936 – JUNE 1972

And if Hamlet had come to the throne?

'Extra! Extra!'
The new King announces:
Victory Square to be re-named after his father;
Ophelia to be buried in holy ground
(The Archbishop agrees);
An amnesty, for all involved in the recent troubles;
A Constitution, modelled on England;
Horatio President of the Council;
Royal Visit to Unemployed;
'Something Must Be Done,' says King.
'Elsinore liberated…a new broom,' report the Ambassadors.
Where ghosts stalked, fireworks.

How many times, since and before,
The new broom? Imaginations that create
From their own staleness a new-born nation;
Acclaim of poets in need of enthusiasm;
Apoplexy of war-heroes, retired honourably
To hunting-lodges in the Lapland forests;
Foreign fashions at Court, the divorcées
Peacocking on the great stairs.

The growlings of the charcoal burners
Will, by the presence at their
Annual Gala of the King himself,
Be somewhat satisfied. News also comes of

Subsidies to the whale-fisheries; this will appease
The truculent North. And for the first time the
Budget is balanced. Many reductions are promised
In the price of essential foods.

And after a while
The country learns of a rival in Hamlet's heart.
Rumours sieved through the palace
Rain on the counting-houses,
Reaching the cottages last.
Goings-on, tales of extravagance;
The old Queen's ruby
Ablaze like Sirius between alien breasts.
The woodcutter is blinded by millions of candles,
Melting the midnight snow, encircling pavilions,
A plumed élite patrol;
And the startled reindeer run south with alarming stories
Of moonlight sleigh-rides, a royal love run wild
Over a laughing face half-hidden in sables.

Bishops are being appointed
For their looks and youth alone;
Schools left half-built for caskets from Paris;
A hospital sacrificed to pay for a banquet
For a new ally (Horatio sidestepped),
Whom the Council have not approved. Demonstrations,
About rising prices. Arrests.
The Constitution withdrawn.
Appeals,
Petitions,
Answered with masques and fêtes.

Till it ends as it ended before,
'Extra! Extra!
Horatio Resigns!'

Fortinbras has been summoned
To restore the old values, establish discipline,
Expel the musicians, supply confidence to the Army.

It will have given the people something to talk about,
A scandal more interesting than the price of meat,
In which a reduction is promised.
The veteran Marshal
Resumes his sword, shakes out a mothy pelisse,
And offers his services to the new dynasty.
And on the frontier
A coach with the blinds drawn down
And a few horsemen are crossing to a farewell salvo
For a promising Prince, a brilliant spinner of words.

Sad, sad, it was only words.

Of King Edward VIII, in exile Duke of Windsor. It happened in 1936. I wrote the poem after 1972, when he died in Paris. My father, as Secretary to the Duchy of Cornwall, saw a good deal of him as Duke, and was summoned, with the King's three brothers, to witness the Deed of Abdication, signed at Fort Belvedere, his 'toy castle' near Ascot, on my twenty-fourth birthday. I saw something of the Abdication myself, not so close-to, but as a fly in the corridors of power. I had just joined The Times. *Geoffrey Dawson, the editor, was the most powerful voice in the Press determined that the King should not be allowed to marry Mrs Simpson and remain on the throne. Mr Deakin being away, I sat in his place at the afternoon conferences, Dawson presiding, and learned a little of what was going on behind the scenes. I enjoyed, in the poem, imagining the whole drama transferred to Elsinore, and the King as a kind of Hamlet; only, however, 'kind of', since he had very little of Hamlet's Renaissance culture and was never the 'brilliant spinner of words' I made of my Hamlet. But there was something in an exclamation he may be remembered for that had a very strong echo in an experience of my own about the same time. During his years as Prince of Wales he had acquired popularity. In that winter of 1936 he had paid a visit to the coalfields of South Wales, where there was mass unemployment, and been photographed surrounded by out-of-work miners. Appalled by what he saw, he had said, and the words had been headlined in every newspaper, 'Something must be done.' Two weeks later he had given up the throne for Mrs Simpson. My father, who had liked and been intensely loyal to him, seldom spoke of him afterwards. I have no published record of what the miners thought, but the poem ends: 'Sad, sad, it was only words'.*

4
Overblest

Sleep, little Prince, in your lace.
The Good Fairies' gifts are all given.
One gave a beautiful face,
Another a shapely figure,
A third a tremendous inheritance,
Four health and five added vigour;

And the last has promised intelligence
Of the highest possible rating.
Lucky boy, you've the world at your feet.
So why are we waiting?
The christening isn't complete.
We're expecting the Wicked Fairy.

She's never been late before.
It's been one of her odious whims,
Old Frau Snake-in-the-Grass,
To stand at the back and malevolently

Cackle at the top brass,
Then chant rude words to the hymns,

Before she delivers her curse.
Once it was constipation.
Once, an irremovable wart.
She destroyed one babe by bestowing
A sexual deviation
Of a highly embarrassing sort.

A horseman! O, what does he bring
For the little Prince's undoing
In that note from the Bad to the Good?
'Count me out' is what she has written.
'All the damage that do you could
You have done, and I'm not needed.'

I had had the King in mind (apart from, in his case, 'intelligence of the highest possible rating') and with him other men and women in that world (though none with a comparable 'tremendous inheritance'). Influence by one of these on my behalf had helped me to my job on The Times, *that led to my next poem.*

5
The Canadian Arctic, 1939

I piloted a packing-case,
Shirt-sleeved above the snow.
Not everyone has been sunburned
At twenty-five below.

Pursuing to the gold-mine
The white Mackenzie's lead,
I dipped to Yellowknife and made
The buffalo stampede.

The tartan-hooded pioneers
Lit fires beneath the screw.
My fingers froze on door-handles.
I dined on caribou.

Two prostitutes across a lake
Had made a hut their home.
A grub who'd drunk away his stake
Inquired when war would come

To hoist him from the tundra
And back to Scotland soon,
And ruined Indians slouched the ice.
Like jackals on the moon.

In 1939 the newspaper sent me on a journey across Canada to commission articles for a Canadian supplement, preparatory to reporting the projected journey of the new King George VI and his Queen Elizabeth, which would also take in Washington and New York and a meeting with Franklin and Eleanor Roosevelt. At Edmonton on the first journey I met Leigh Brintnell, who was running a pioneer air-service to open up the hitherto little-known Far North. He took me with him and let me take control of the plane. I reported the opening of the first gold-mine at Yellowknife (hence the 'packing-case', the grub-staker homesick for Scotland, and the 'ruined Indians'). The royal tour was a success from start to finish and made a world star for the rest of her life of the Queen, later Queen Mother. I remember, but have no poem on which to hang them, the welcoming crowds coast-to-coast in Canada, even tiny groups at whistle-stop halts after nightfall; the scene at Washington's grave; the cavalry procession along Pennsylvania Avenue; the crowds lining the shores of Halifax harbour singing 'Will ye no' come back again'; and finally the dark underside of Empire in Newfoundland, where a poverty-stricken village mainly on relief had raised an arch of branches with a banner painted 'Paradise Welcomes Their Majesties'.

6
Until That Night

This is an extract from a long poem, published in 1953. I made this extract in 2004. 'That night' means 28/29 March 1942, the night of the assault on St Nazaire. In the long poem I had been describing Hitler's armies as they swept across Europe, turning it into a forest fire aswarm with

cobras, wood by wood,
Where no birds sang, no love could suck
The poison from that swaying hood.
Many centuries' disease
Hungered howling for release.
It had to strike, and when it struck
Many light hearts loved I found
Like bright springs forced underground;
Swallows, who thought the sea a lake, and drowned.

They and I had compasses in our hands,
Stumbling at night through ploughland, safe at home,
Ringing through towns and falling asleep in barns,
On sacks of hay,
At the end of a make-believe day.

They and I in boats slipped wrists of channels,
Slithering through across the grating shoals,
Watching for pinprick torches on practice beaches,
Then stealing ashore, like spies,
Through waves waist-high,

Before the horizon was slit for the pearl of morning,
Before the smokewreath rose from whitewashed farms,
To be inland away like thieves to supposed objectives,
Padding with squelchy feet
Through heather and peat.

I was there in all that pretence, that youth, that training,
On perpendicular rocks, in seas, in Hebrides,
Refreshing with cheerful voices numberless places,
Voices soon stilled,
Place that would never be filled...
March day and night that altered me,
Sea that we crossed, far more than sea,
Enemy more than enemy.

Now the life I lived before
Rekindles into metaphor.
With them the common purpose won,
Shall it survive, now they are gone,
All that I learnt, all I once taught,
To storm an artificial fort,
Assure a bridgehead, seize a beach,
Become with whom to learn or teach
Relevant to the long default
In man's historical assault?

Morning was their burial pall.
All as one, one most of all,
Haunting down the ten-year past,
Tell us what today has lost.

Sunrise was sunset for thee.
Now all grow timeless; like the sea,
From whose heart, that took them, throng
Thoughts as long as our lives are long.

Wild-wagered youth, call, cause, crusade,
What a world we might have made!

The poem is about our training before the assault as much as the assault itself. Out of the twenty-five from the troop who came with me to St Nazaire, fifteen were killed. But the assault succeeded. Many experts thought it impossible. On its fortieth anniversary, in honour of the killed, the present Queen Elizabeth invited our Society of survivors to return to St Nazaire in the royal yacht Britannia. *It was an imaginative and just tribute. Recalling what I think of as 'the Commando spirit', so democratic, so light-hearted, so ready to take on anything, I came to believe, and still believe, that nothing worth accomplishing, whether on a much larger scale or in individual obscurity, is impossible. Years later, during times of nationwide disillusion, I added the last two lines to the end of 'Until That Night'.*

7
Endymion Talks to the Press

'The greatest week in History!'
I don't think!
'Didn't I rage?' you ask me.
'Wasn't my nose
Put out of joint by those heroes
(Heroes indeed!)

Blundering trampolining
All over the moon.
My moon!
I'll give you my answer. Exit.
And soon, I hope. Just as soon
As the first moon-liner leaves,
I shall go with it.
Admitted, I have been shaken.
After staring more than two thousand
Years, understand,
At an image of perfect purity,
To learn
She is not
Even, possibly never was,
Inviolable,
Had, possibly, mortals of some kind on her before,
But to me, whatever else happened to her,
Is dead,
I need to die.
That's why
I've booked. And I hope we crash.
I can't cope
With another two thousand
Staring at Earth,
Or staying on Earth. Understand,
I've seen Earth,
Lived Earth. I know what you call Humanity.

If we don't crash, I shall stay there,
As far as I can get from the coke-swilling passengers.
Better for me,
Dreamer, whose lifelong craving
Has been to be numbered
Among the immortal
High Priests of the Ideal,
To die on an only slightly encumbered-

With-hardware breast, and caress
Bits of a once beautiful, pure, dead mistress,
Than start again with another,
Who's not only alive but raving,
Thank you for coming to see me.'

I wrote this after the Americans had landed on the moon. The contrast between it and the next poem (8) is the reason for including both here. Poem 7 is the statement of an embittered cynic. In the original Greek myth, or one version of it, Endymion had been a beautiful mortal youth, immortalised by love for the Moon. The Moon was his Ideal; he was content to spend eternity gazing at her. Now the Americans had landed on her, and who could say what might follow? She had been desecrated. He could not anyhow remain on earth. Earth had been desecrated long ago. The only way for him was suicide.

8

To the Moon

Time,
Isn't it,
Time to get on?
The weir unwinds the linoleum river.
The clock-face reddens...
Why are you sitting here,
Sitting and staring here,
In this high window, gaping for dividends still
From a bankrupt estate, still banging a broken-down till,
Still groping wistfully
For a worn fantasy,
And a pocked goddess?

Smudge, thumbprint, fingernail;
Snowball or puffball; dumpling; immaculate snail;
Melon; or monk's bald patch;
Egg, or top of an egg; escaped balloon;
The moon, the moon,

Parthenon on the rock of Heaven;
Jib on a black lagoon;
Like a pierrot left outside
When the folds of the curtain join;
Like a woman who dances for love
In the wood, in the shadowy park
When the theatres are all destroyed,
Pavlova of the dark.

Like a poet in a white shirt
Lying dead on a battlefield;
Like a bundle of rags lying motionless
When the soldiers have cleared the square...

Come, captain pen, enough of reveries!
I meant to raise my voice against wicked men.
Against men of spite, against cruel men.
Back to our enemies!
Though there came to my window last night a beautiful
    face,
All roads they march, and we...must find our place.

I found 'To the Moon' almost forgotten among my first collection, published by Rupert Hart-Davis in 1953. It was written in Colditz. It is the statement of someone determined to get on with things. He starts by rounding on his own dreaminess and idleness: 'Why are you sitting here...?' There follows a catalogue of similes and metaphors for the moon, partly mocking, finally very serious; and the poem ends, 'Come, captain pen, enough of reveries!... All roads they march, and we...must find our place.' Interpreted, the references are: the 'high window' is the barred and floodlit window of the games room in Colditz; the 'bankrupt estate' something to do with pre-war Britain; the 'broken-down till' with capitalism, whether State- or market-driven; and the 'bundle of rags' a memory, at the time I wrote it a foretelling, of that unforgettable photograph of a lone Chinese youth opposing the leading tank sent in to clear Tienanman Square in Beijing in 1989. The poet in a white shirt is the Hungarian national hero-poet Petöfi Sandor, who will be found later in Group Two. 'All roads they march' means the battlefields raging all over the world outside Colditz. And 'our place'? My place, for the time, was Colditz, where I was safe and could go politically to the Left in peace.

9
The View from the Castle

Leaden tongues of summer
Licking streets and roof.
Only brainless starlings
Feel the need to move.

Houses like hot tombs.
People, are they dead,
Strolling from their homes,
Crossing strips of shade?

One of these full noons
Everything will stop.
One such sluggish summer
Time and town will drop,

Like a purple rose
Flopping from a sill.
Drop into the river,
Moving without will.

Only in the square.
All the livelong day,
Something in themselves
Makes the fountains play.

Only from the heart
Comes the thudding call.
Like a wireless clock
Through an empty hall.

10
Colditz

I was a prisoner in a cobweb keep,
Or like a prince, who in the mirror sees
Invading hosts, and frets, and cannot sleep,
And wrings his hands, and falls upon his knees,
Now running to the glass with feverish looks,
To find his soldiers flung from lost positions;
Now with pale fingers fluttering old books
For spells not there, and fled are the magicians.
Follows the quiet when false fear surrenders,
When what's to come is not yet come, but must;
When what he had is no more worth defenders,
And rank and robe as barren as the dust.
Camouflage gone, he is as he began,
Not pale nor prince, nor prisoner, but a man.

I did not try to escape myself. I did my military duty, keeping watch on the movements of sentries and suchlike activities, to help my companions in some of their astonishing escapes. I saw it as my role to study, not just how to get out of the castle and home to fight again, but how we had got there in the first place. Why there had been a war at all? Why any war? What sort of society to work for once we had been liberated? What had my friends died for? Thanks to the Geneva Convention, which the Germans observed (until the end, when the SS took over from the Wehrmacht), and to our Protecting Power, the Swiss, I was able to get books to study, not literature but economics, which I detest; and, while still a prisoner, obtained a diploma in Social Studies 'with distinction in all subjects' at Oxford University, that made up for the degree in 'Greats' I had shirked while there. I lectured and wrote two books, one of which, a long novel called Yes, Farewell, *based on Colditz (under another name) and all but finished there, came out immediately after the war, long before the place became a household word. Jonathan Cape published the novel, Rupert Hart-Davis published the other book, a long poem I wrote almost straight down while semi-delirious in the sick ward, called* The Flying Castle. *I imagined a violent storm getting under the foundations and lifting it, complete with guards and prisoners, on a mad journey through the sky. Michael Russell republished it as an appendix to my autobiography; it describes the kind of journey many writers must have longed for and has never come to me again. My feet the rest of the time were kept very much on the ground, though potentially dangerous ground; my fellow prisoners did me the honour, as an experienced journalist knowing shorthand, of trusting me to take down the precious BBC news at the side of the wireless officer, from the set hidden in the eaves of one of the Castle's enormous attics.*

My studies were a privilege, part of a respite, albeit too long and enforced by prison, which does not come to many; a time to look back on and ponder my life before, my mistakes and aspirations, and consider what I might do about them in the future. I had just reached thirty: Dante's 'nel mezzo del cammin di nostra vita', *'in the midway of this our mortal life', not, or only occasionally, to study the road to a Paradiso hereafter, but how to make happier places like that poverty-stricken Paradise village in Newfoundland that had welcomed the King and Queen. Events had driven my aspirations beyond cures for unemployment to other wrongs concerning peace, democracy, liberty.*

Up in the attic I listened not only to the BBC, but to the thunder of Stalin's Orders of the Day saluting massive victories and, in all, twenty million deaths. My lectures turned into Marxism with a strong bias in its favour, and were listened to and answered. In this sense as in others, signally unrecognised in the welter of publicity over nearly half a century, Colditz held a faint candle of democratic liberty in a continent sodden with tyranny and lies.

In one aspect it was a microcosm of society before the war, especially at the extreme ends. At the most elevated end was the mess-table to which, rather to my surprise, I had been allocated. Most of my messmates had been at Eton. Several were regular soldiers, captured in the first days of the war, victims of the disgraceful Thirties, brought to Colditz for successive attempts to escape. Two or three of aristocratic or royal blood, like a handful in other messes, were being held under special watch, obviously as hostages, and in daily danger. They accepted me and trusted me with the secret news, as they had already accepted Giles Romilly, Winston Churchill's nephew and a member of the British Communist Party. All are now dead, and I miss their courage and their tolerance. At the opposite end of the social scale, in a different mess, was Dusty Miller, son of a working member of the Boilermakers' Union, and before the war active in the Young Communist League. To Dusty (christened Norman) I dedicated the following poem 'Sleep for Now'.

II

Sleep for Now

FOR DUSTY MILLER

Sleep for now, secure from struggle;
From the unachieved delight;
From the fever, the disfavour;
From the victory, from the rout;
In oblivion, in assurance,
Let the dreams and demons out.

Sleep, and in the mindless country,
For an hour forget the wish,
Unremitted, unrequited,
For a gentler life to live,
For a far less fierce tomorrow
Than today can gauge, or give.

Sleep, and sails on the horizon,
Trumpets, armies in the hills,
Not divert you, not disturb you,
On whose head the half-light falls,
While the panthers of the morning
Steal their paws along the walls.

Sleep, and through the grateful watcher,
Though I hear the break of doom,
Flows a quiet from your quiet,
Like an unimpassioned tune
Underneath the walls of trouble.
Inaccessible, immune.

He had run away to sea in his early teens and begun his working career washing dishes in the steerage galley of a luxury transatlantic liner. He had come to Colditz by way of the Merchant Navy and then as a sub-lieutenant engineer in the Royal Navy, on board a ship sunk in an Atlantic convoy. Picked out of the ocean and made a prisoner of war, he had escaped. He became my closest friend. I taught him economics. The friendship lasted until his death in 1985. Over all that time, beginning in the Castle's enforced cloisterhood, he taught me the realities of working-class life, glimpsed hitherto in peacetime from a distance. Nearly all the prisoners slept in dormitories on straw palliasses in double-tier bunks. Near the end of the war he and I were in the same room, on lower bunks opposite one another. Unable to sleep one dawn, I watched him as he lay asleep and some lines began to come to me. The Americans advancing to liberate us from the west, the Russians from the east, turned into

> *... sails on the horizon,*
> *Trumpets, armies,*
> *Not divert you, not disturb you ...*

Thinking of the job ready for me on The Times, *with other possibilities, and all the many securities of status, I contrasted them with what would be awaiting him. For him peace would mean the old competitive struggle, insecurity, the cost of starting a family, finding a home, even (as after World War One) a return to unemployment and the dole. I wished him 'Sleep' in order ' for an hour' to 'forget the wish', that had no comparable urgency for me:*

> *For a gentler life to live,*
> *For a far less fierce tomorrow*
> *Than today can gauge, or give.*

Elsewhere, at greater length, I have described Dusty's influence on my longing 'to strike some blow' against social injustice. In this note I shall pass to the next poem and his place in the narrative of my other longing: 'for requited love'. He was several years younger, handsome, and irrevocably heterosexual. I had had one happy but inconclusive affair with an older woman and begun to think myself irrevocably what was not yet called ' gay'. I have also written, also elsewhere, how, nonetheless, I imagined a profound experience with a woman and, finally, life with a woman to be 'one of the immortal openings into life'. To Dusty, experienced in affairs with the opposite sex, I showed the next poem.

12
For Dinah

They come from refreshing hills.
Foreign women in bright shawls,
Down white and winding roads
Out of the spring woods.

You were a girl with light-
Brown hair and light-brown eyes.
Wherever you went you left
A wish, a catch in the breath.

Walk again through the people
Like a child in a dour temple,
Making the roué, the wraith,
Bitterly think of his youth;

Making whoever begs
Bitterly think of his rags.
I that have been your foil,
Turning my face to the wall,

Feel an impossible breath,
Hear an implacable scythe,

Swishing and slashing away.
Never a reason why.

They come from renewing hills,
Foreign women in bright shawls,
Making these growing woods
Wanted, and changed my roads.

Dusty listened, listened with understanding I badly needed at the time, to the story of Dinah's relationship with me, which compelled that poem. More than any girl I have met, she seems today the one whose looks, spirit, innocence and tragedy most recall love-poetry in past centuries; I see her quite easily as Juliet, or a girl in a folk-song. First memories and photographs of her come from carefree days in 1935, staying at her parents' home in Norfolk when she was eighteen and I twenty-two. One photograph shows her playing the guitar in front of a portrait of an ancestress. She excelled at it and during the war sang to it at concerts with her elder sister. There is a strangely long gap in my memories until the war. In the summer of 1941 she came to stay with me when I was training with 2 Commando at Moffat in Dumfriesshire. She had a room next to me at the Star Hotel which, with the permission, even participation, of Mr and Mrs Butler the owner-managers, my troop once barricaded and used in a mock exercise. There is a photograph of Dinah, elsewhere, radiant on the Commando sports day. Before leaving she told me of her love, which had lasted since our first meeting. She had had admirers and offers of marriage, but had refused them and never taken a lover. I told her of my predominant homosexuality. In a letter on her return home she required a letter 'as honest and cruel and bare as you can'. After I had obliged, we began a correspondence. She wrote long, wonderful letters, in high, sloping handwriting, filling the page with dashes instead of punctuation; wise far beyond her years, witty, with drawings that would have assured her a livelihood as a caricaturist; sometimes, inevitably, sad, with a sadness she strove to make no more than rueful. But once, in a letter near despair, she wrote as if our association was at an end, 'With the war so near I wish I was your mistress and had your child.'

In January 1942, thinking the Commando, still restlessly training in Scotland, would never be sent into action, and hoping to be parachuted into France, I got a job at SOE HQ in London. I was able to see Dinah often. My mother loved her and longed for us to marry. We managed one idyllic, or all-but idyllic, weekend staying with Molly Berkeley at Berkeley Castle, where I had spent several weekends while apprenticed to the Gloucester Citizen *The castle was almost all under dust-sheets, Molly looking after old Lord Berkeley in a few small rooms. I went for a walk with Dinah alongside a small stream and she sang some of her French songs. In London it soon became clear that, for some time anyhow, I would be retained in an office collating reports from secret agents in Europe instead of hiding there and sending them. I wanted to return to the Commandos and told Dinah. Of course, she wrote to me, she wanted me to stay in London, 'but I can't argue that because of it'; and then, in words I could never easily forget, 'Don't deceive yourself, whatever you choose. Don't pretend – like well-meaning Governments, it reminds me of Appeasement. Never that, Micky, never that! Be as true to yourself as you can be and don't force anything ... to please me ... and you can never know what pleases me – that you can't control!'*

I went back. On the night before I left, I took Dinah to 10 Buckingham Gate, my father's office and our peacetime home opposite Buckingham Palace. Part of it had been torn down by a bomb and my parents had moved to the suburbs. I was staying and sleeping in a room left habitable. Dinah and I spent the night together there, and I failed her. I said goodbye outside her parents' flat. More than half a century later I learnt from one of her sisters that she had been in tears and told her she had been with me 'and everything had gone wrong and I shall never see him again'. I became a prisoner of war that night, 28/29 March 1942. I wrote to her, but had no reply. One day in June 1943 I had a letter in my first P.O.W. camp (before I was transferred to Colditz) from my mother, telling me that Dinah had died the previous Christmas Eve, of tuberculosis.

All this I related to Dusty when I got to Colditz. I told him also that I had had no inkling she was ill. And I remembered one of the French songs she had sung walking with me that day beside the stream in Gloucestershire. It was a love-song about a girl called Madeleine. In the first verse the lover recalled seeing her for the first time, young and wearing a white dress; and in the last she was still young, but the white dress was for her funeral; and the refrain of each verse was 'Que les beaux jours sont courts'.

Dusty, next Morgan Jenkins, Dinah, finally Mary, are all linked, physically, actually linked in their lives by a succession of coincidences, as I now deliberately link them in this first group of poems. Morgan, the Welsh beau chevalier, our Richard Burton, who used to take off his subaltern's pips to go out with the 'other ranks' from among whom he had been promoted, was also killed. I remember a night in 1941 when both of us were on leave from Scotland. He had told me he would like to see something of 'the posh world'. So I took Dinah and him to dinner at the Dorchester. It was a wonderfully happy evening. While they were talking I looked past them across the crowded tables; and there on the dance-floor was the most beautiful woman I had ever seen. I followed her with my eyes when the music stopped. She was with a party and I felt I would never see her again. Next day Charles Haydon, the brigadier in charge of the Commandos at Combined Operations, asked some of us to a drink at his flat. I rang the bell and the same woman opened the door. Her name was Mary; Charles was her first cousin. I told her of the coincidence and have repeated it in two books and to many people. I was taken prisoner soon afterwards. In April 1945, liberated from Colditz, I sent her a stilted little note, reminding her. She answered and I called on her. We began to meet daily. I told her of my sexual misgivings and we fell in love.

13

Most Happy Creature

Today there's not a feature
That goes against my nature.
I'm the world's most happy creature.

Don't ask me for the reason
For being out of season.
Even now, upon occasion,

The wheels are in connection.
The world's the rhythm section,
And I'm the trumpet section.

Confusion may come later.
Today it's not my nature.
I'm the world's most happy creature.

I think of this poem as written the day after Mary and I first made love, in Sussex, and the times that followed soon afterwards, in Wales, when I believed that my sexual problems were at an end. Academically, the lines may interest those curious to know the origins of love-poems, indeed of any poems. One evening in the castle, Jimmy Yule, one of the officers in charge of the secret radio, and I, his shorthand writer, had gone up to the attic to take the BBC. We squeezed ourselves into the hide early by accident, in time to hear a jazz pianist. Jimmy, an expert on jazz, was thrilled. He told me the pianist was called Fats Waller and world famous, and I pretended to have heard of him. He played so brilliantly and joyously round that reiterated last line, that the same night, after I had deciphered my notes and given the news out to the heads of sleeping-quarters, I built a poem of my own round it, making it the third line in mine, now, sixty years later, reproduced opposite. I met Jimmy after the war and reminded him of the occasion, and he told me I had written the pianist's name down as 'Fat Swallow'. The lines had no connection with Colditz, except that I wrote them there, and nothing to do with Mary, whom I had scarcely met at the time.

GROUP TWO

Mary was forty-four when I first saw her, and I not quite twenty-nine. To the end of her life the word most commonly used about her beauty was 'timeless'. The first poems that follow are among the first I wrote to and for her, in Wales before our marriage and afterwards in Vienna and Budapest, where The Times *sent me as their resident correspondent. I arrived in Vienna on the very day that Churchill made his speech at Fulton in the USA about the Iron Curtain descending over Central and Eastern Europe. Stalin answered it a few days later, and the Cold War started. Mary joined me first in Vienna and then from 1947 till the autumn of 1949 we lived in Budapest, and I reported the descent of the Curtain over Hungary.*

14
Words Sent Out

Words few will find homes for,
Go out and get lost
Small words, pointless as humming-birds
In the kestrel sky, go out.
No one will think you worth killing.

Time with its sullenness
The clearest lineaments to vagueness turns,
Her dearest voice will blur,
Splinter the glass, the echo dissipate,
What most seemed sure, disturb.

Who knows this, will receive you,
Words of no moment, love-birds,
Fledged by the rainbow years.

15
I Thought, 'New Styles'

I thought, 'New styles'.
'Modern' of course,
Prepared to pack
My wooden horse,

And reconnoitred
The weakest way
To infiltrate
The Muses' Troy.

I planned to ring
The sacred bells
Of X and Y
And other swells,

Then run away,
And leave behind
A grinning scarecrow
For them to find.

In face of tears
Would not unbend,
And spice my lyrics
With an acid end;

Spoil with a sponge
The heroic entrance,
And strew with tintacks
The lovers' dance;

The maestro's Hessians
Smear with glue,
And Juliet's balcony
Saw half through.

What has happened?
I am loved. I love,
And cannot quit
The romantic groove,

And am debarred
From certain poses,
Not in the mood
To make long noses.

16

A Young Bird

A young bird fell from its nest.
It lay the shape of my heart,
Silent, peaked, without feathers,
And scrawny, with straight stiff feet.

What, of you or the world,
Thought had so clogged my mind
That while I slept I dreamed
You wept for that small bird;

And I took up one of your tears
To put in the rigid beak,
And the featherless body stirred,
And the heart began to beat.

17
As an Old Scholar

As an old scholar fumbles a new book,
Coming on honeycombs he fancied spent
Humming, hearing again
Sicilian sounds, the warm, the world's youth's strains,
Theocritus, and smiles, and is content,
And dies,
This evening dies.

As an old priest, tired out with answering
Other men's fears, and hungry to be blest
Himself, points steepled palms
Transparent to the everlasting arms,
And hears the shore calling the shell to rest,
And dies,
This evening dies.

Grey clouds and red caress the sky's blue face.
The poplars shiver. Summer's flowers close.
Quiet moves down
Even among the birds, and in the town
The rose of evening makes the ruins rose.
And I,
Who do not die,

And thought of it too long, and do not now,
And am not such a man, scholar or priest,
Watch where you move, you float,
Among the flowers in a long white coat,
Thinking of loveliness and love at least
In you,
And all you do.

18
Exempted

She sits in front of her glass,
Leaning her cheek on her hand, a little morose,
And says, 'My lines are all going downward.'
She does not know what I know
Of the compact of Time with Beauty
To continue his task, the part he cannot evade,
And yet to concede
For this exceptional one, not as a precedent,
Since lines must come, come then as a setting for jewels
Or faint as the gossamer lines
On a perfectly mended bowl;
If the body's strength must grow less, then to pass
Into the spirit, the soul,
And to show
In the eyes, that may glitter no more, but shall glow.

So she sits in front of her glass,
Takes off her make-up, ties her hair,
And comes to bed,

Little knowing she has been watching a miracle.

19
Ecology

When the pipeline gasps for oil,
When the ores are down to bone,
No more copper, no more nitrates,
Warmth and light and telephone

More than halfway back to Newton,
Horse and cart and no more coal,
Farmers chopping down the orchards
For a fire to fry a mole;

When the gentlemen and ladies,
In that pinched millennium,
Riot round the herring trawlers,
Won't another shortage come

In that worn and torn tomorrow,
Worse than running-down supplies?
Even she will have grown older,
Even her oasis eyes

Have less strength to sweeten deserts,
Take the tears and solaced send
Children home, and others older,
Bringing broken hearts to mend.

Earth, what will you do without her
When the fevers vainly call,
When the heartache gets no answer.
When she has no strength at all?

Solar tappings, tidal voltage,
May the oracles of waste disprove,
No laboratory replenish
Such a deficit of love.

20

A War Story

There was this train, he told me,
Clanking west to the front
Through trees like snow pagodas.
Russia in 'forty-three.

All the soldiers were young
Peasants sprawling on straw
In cattle-trucks big as ballrooms.
In one a lantern swung

Like a ship's in a slight swell.
On grey greatcoats, on cropped heads
Boxed inside fur ear-flaps
Its thin light rose and fell,

While the muttonchop *starshina*,
Grandfather of the regiment,
Told stories of his boyhood…
'I remember in Georgia,

When the good king died, his brother
Took the queen and the throne,
And a ghost appeared to the son…'
'You're muddled, grandfather,'

One of them pipes up.
'That's a play...by William Shakespeare,
An English writer...in school...'
'Hold your tongue, you young pup!

I'm speaking of people I've seen.
There was a chief too, the witches
Told he'd be king, and his woman
Fancied herself as queen.

So they slit the old king's throat.
And there was a silly old peasant
Got his cattle and household together
And kept them on board a boat,

Because he expected a flood.
And a kitchen-girl married a prince,
And a sultan dressed up as a beggar...'
Tales from a far childhood

In a westward-jogging train
Under a swinging lantern
For soldiers sprawling on straw
Who'll never stack straw again.

And I thought of a train jogging east,
Sealed too, but not against weather,
With a rabbi repeating stories
Of a hand at a royal feast,

That wrote some words on a wall,
And a prophet who spoke with God,
For another truckload of people
Who are also beyond recall,

And how I might tell of those two
Trains one day for a story,
And a boy would pipe up and say,
'Grandfather, it's not true.'

This derives from a story told us in Vienna by Ernst Fischer, the chief and only outstanding figure in the Austrian Communist Party, who became a friend of ours. He and his wife Ruth had escaped from Austria after the defeat of the Social Democrat Party in 1934 and spent the rest of the war among the crowds of Communist and Socialist refugees in the Soviet Union, about whom he had fascinating stories. He visited the battlefronts during the war, questioning and doing propaganda among the Austrian prisoners. It was during one of these journeys that he shared a cattle-truck conveying a company of Russian soldiers to their regiment at the front, and heard the old patriarch of a sergeant-major (the starshina, *with mutton-chop side-whiskers) telling them the story of Hamlet as if it had happened during his own childhood at home. The picture, as Ernst described it, was Homeric. I added the train going in the opposite direction, taking Jews to the gas chambers.*

Ernst accepted obedience to Stalin with the contention, as he explained to me, that 'in this age the western intellectual, with his higher culture, sensitivity, and discrimination, has to yield his admiration and support to a primitive people, who have initiated the most advanced of all social experiments'. He hung on to this belief longer than many European Communists who felt the same, but the Soviet invasion of Czechoslovakia and end of the 'Prague spring' were too much for him. He was expelled from the Communist Party and, as a gifted author and critic, became an influence in what was once, perhaps many times, called the New Left. He died in the early Seventies. His autobiography stays in my mind. John Berger wrote an affectionate and moving preface.

21
Alexander Petöfi

An eagle, a Magyar eagle,
Soared from the plains,
Golden in the dust
Mirages of the Alföld.

Breaker of horses, tamer
Of Pegasus, hobo
Scholar and stroller player.

Lover of women, then
Of one only, lastly
Lay down with Freedom.
Byron in rags, eighteen forty-eight
Revolutionary.

The lancers spiked him.

Dip, feathers of gold, over Segesvar's
Last stand,
The blood-soaked tunic
And twenty-six years
Of Petöfi Sandor.

Found earth glorious, and sang.
Adored life, gave it.

Alexander Petöfi (Petöfi Sandor, 1823–49), Hungary's national poet, disowned by a tyrannical father, led the wretched life of a strolling player for three years, with an interval as a common soldier in an infantry regiment to escape starvation. His first collection of lyrical, martial and patriotic poems, published when he was twenty-four and poverty-stricken, met with enthusiasm from the public and one or two poets and critics, but with cold dislike from the established classicists. When the Revolution of 1848 broke out he joined the army of another true Hungarian hero, Josef Bem, whom he immortalised in his poetry. He rose by sheer valour to the rank of major and was killed at the Battle of Segesvar, fighting the massed armies of Austria and Russia. Bem escaped by pretending to be dead. (Petöfi's body was never found. A story, from Russian sources, has recorded his death as a prisoner in Russia, but Hungarian authorities have told me it is not believed in Hungary.) Petöfi, to our shame, is little known in the United Kingdom. I think of him as one of the few great poets and revolutionary romantics who was actually killed in battle. His biography became the life-work of Lajos Hatvany, the Hungarian millionaire-born but rebel patron of two other illustrious poets, Ady and Attila Josef. Hatvany was driven into exile and later imprisoned by the Horthy government in the Twenties, and spent the 1939–45 war in lodgings in Oxford, exiled for the second time. He returned to Budapest and finished the biography, in five volumes, just before he died. Something about him and his no less amazing wife Loli is in my autobiography.

22

The Workman on the Danube Bridge

I made this bridge,
I raised it, raised it,
From mud, from mud,
And the river that ran with blood.

Mine were the arms
That held it, held it;
My thighs the vice
That clenched it from the groaning ice.

Sinew and steel,
I stood, bridge stood,
And braced our back
Against the thaw, and did not crack.

The sly old stream,
In one mood never
One moment stays,
And ambushed me on windy days.

The derricks dipped.
The river smiled.
On rib and rung
I perched, and in the rigging hung.

Aloft, assured,
I held, I hammered
Girders and chains,
And caught them from the floating cranes;

And whistled back
At wrestling winds
That sought to throw
My body to the friend below.

Best were the days,
Dangling my legs
In shine and sun,
In summer, with a section done.

But long the hours
To end it, end it;
The lamp's blue spark
Bored on and burnt into the dark.

Heavy the work,
Wide, wide the river.
An impulse new,
Delighted with a distant view,

Drew shore to shore.
I joined them, joined them,
With side and span,
A steel anatomy of man.

And now the world
May gladly ride,
Or sadly march
Across the rainbow-perfect arch.

I raised this bridge.
I laid it, made it.
Gulfs are divine.
God put them there. The bridge is mine.

The next three poems, 'Farewell to Hungary', 'Budapest 1949' and 'A Window in Buda' are the final outcome of my disillusion there, as I witnessed the takeover of the country by the Communist Party, under the 'protection' of the victorious Red Army.

23
Farewell to Hungary

I have learned from people who had bleeding feet,
And tattered coats, and faces like old maps,
And doffed their hats when one went past like me.

They crouched by hedges with a beast's despair,
Without the resignation of the beasts,
Tamed by speech and yet unable to speak.

Their women were cowed, their opinions never sought.
They served at table when a stranger came,
Withering like stalks that no one asks for a leaf.

Bending among the corn like knotted trees,
They broke their backs in service of two lords,
Men far away, and earth, that never reprieves.

I waited, and saw the fuses fiercely laid
To these walls of body and mind, and all released
In huge and terrible flowers over the earth,

And a spark has fallen upon me, and touched a charge,
As if the words had been Arabs champing within me,
Tethered too long by grooms who muffled their feet.

Their homes will have lights, the daughter who leaves will teach,
She who remains will read, and smooth be her cheek.
I have seen their banners ablaze in the mariner wheat.

I have tried to forget the prisons, but I cannot.
Vengeance was yours. I remember, dumb with defeat,
The guiltless faces. Hungary, by this beach

I shall remember you, in this English clearing,
And in my mind forever flows the Tisza,
And in my heart forever grind your keys

There is a Hungarian proverb, 'He who once drinks out of the Tisza always has a longing to go back' i.e. return to his native land of Hungary, or just to Hungary. The Tisza is a river flowing into the Danube in Eastern Hungary. I did drink out of it, and did go back, but not until the forty years of the Cold War were over.

24
Budapest 1949

The ragged town below me,
With sores on every wall,
Plucks at the cloud-grained heavens,
And there the world goes well.

Along their placid reaches
The constants swanlike sail.
They brush the beggared houses,
And there the world goes ill.

The poet chucks his coins
Out of a hopeful till.
He cannot understand it
If no one hears them fall.

Three milk-white goats came by me,
Lying sad upon the hill.
If they took me for a plant,
I did not break the spell.

The town beneath, I lay there,
The sky above, until
I felt them crop behind my cheek
And heard their footsteps small.

Well, let them crop my head, I said.
Today it's far too full.
Today let men be tortured.
I will not hear them call.

25
A Window in Buda 1951–1989

IN MEMORY OF GIZI BAJOR, ACTRESS,
AND TIBOR GERMAN, SURGEON

Drums, drums across the Danube!
Banners. A Birnam wood.
Not coming for us, though.
We aren't the Macbeths.

More banners. A demonstration.
Will you ride to meet them, dearest,
In the scarlet robe you wore
When you stunned them as Mary Stuart?
They will only say you are mad.
And I too mad, to allow you.
Our theatre days are done.

And yet, remember...

Act One:
The Nazis came.
'Your husband's a surgeon?' 'Yes, a famous surgeon.'
'But a Jewish surgeon...' 'No.'
With your husband, as Jewish as anyone,
Under the floorboards, hidden.

Act Two:
The Russians came.
False pouches ageing your eyes,
Made up a hundred and ten,
Quavering, a babuschka:
'Master and mistress have fled. I only work here.'
With your husband hidden again,
Your jewels under their boots,
Under the rose-beds.

Act Three:
To plead for a friend,
You waited on our tyrant,
Our own indigenous home-grown tyrant,
Eyelash black, dressed to kill,
Contraband perfume from a world condemned;
And he saw you, to relish your performance,
And then said, 'No.'

Drums, drums, more banners
Along the renamed boulevards.
The English journalist and his wife
Will have reached Paris by now.
I, who may only visit
Paris without you, or you
Without me, for security,
Shall we put a call through to Paris,
And sit here, listening to the traffic
In Paris? And being listened to,

For security.
'They are saying nothing to Paris.
What kind of code is that?'

Come in, dear. Close the curtains.
Theatre is down there.
Big theatre.
A major operating theatre.
Mankind is being re-made.

They are dead by morning.
Official versions have it that she had cancer,
And he couldn't bear it. Others:
They lacked the spirit of the age.
Too private. They did not march.

Years afterwards,
A boy also too private,
Who lacked the spirit of the age,
Set fire to himself. In Prague,
Beside the Wenceslas statue,
His name Jan Palach.
Another not far from Washington,
Whose name I do not know,
Because of Vietnam.

Banners have risen and fallen,
Fallen, risen again.
1956 here.
1968 there.
1989 everywhere.
Write their names on the banners.
Write, though they did not march...
Gizi....Tibor...
Divine art, a healer's skill...
And human love. Farewell.

Gizi Bajor, in memory of whom, with her husband, Tibor German, Poem 25 was written, was a beautiful and warm-hearted woman who had reigned over the Hungarian stage for many years. Tibor was a surgeon of international renown. Mary and I occupied the upper floor of their home on the hills above the Danube during 1947–49 while I was correspondent there. Gizi had played many of the famous parts in comedy and tragedy. The stories in the poem, of how she had hidden Tibor from both the Nazis and, after the long and appalling siege of the city, the Russians, are true. Since the house was not irrevocably damaged during the siege, she had given refuge there to many left destitute; among them Emilia Marcus, mother-in-law of Nijinsky and Gizi's famous predecessor on the stage, whom she had found begging on the streets.

For a while the Hungarian Communists had need of her and Tibor's prestige; neither could get a permit to visit family in the West alone. Gizi enjoyed playing to the new working-class audiences in factories as well as on stage; they were more attentive, she told me, than some of the former fashionable ones had been. But as the regime made its revolutionary intentions more ruthlessly clear, the dispossession or, if they were lucky, the flight of friends westward, distressed her; and also the doctrinaire instructions she was being given by the Party on how certain parts should be interpreted. One woman friend was arrested for an indiscreet remark about the Party Secretary and real dictator of the country, Matyas Rákosi, who in 1947 was beginning a terror that was to last three years. It was for this friend that Gizi went to Rákosi to plead and was rejected. She became La Tosca in real life, not just in an opera. (Hence verse five.)

Mary grew very fond of her; in many ways they were kindred spirits. The day of our final departure was terribly sad. In London Mary had a letter from her, hating her part as Anna Karenina...'Twenty-five scenes. I run around and have no time to feel. I am on the edge of a nervous breakdown...Mary dear, write me a long and big letter to me...' Mary wrote, but it was too late. News came that Gizi and Tibor had been found dead on their bed together.

Some forty years later, after Communism had fallen, and Mary had died, I went back to Budapest. The beautiful house had been turned into a museum of the Hungarian theatre. My poem in English was there in a glass case, alongside its published Hungarian translation, beneath a full-length painting of Gizi in her role as Schiller's Maria Stuart (Mary Queen of Scots). My Mary and I are 'the English journalist and his wife' in the poem. We saw Gizi act once, in a Hungarian translation of a play by the Spanish playwright Lope da Vega. Understanding scarcely a word didn't matter. I remember a moment when the play was brought to a halt by applause not for words, but for a mere gesture of Gizi's. 'To see her on the stage', I wrote for her in The Times, *'was an unforgettable enchantment.'*

'1956' in the poem means the Hungarian revolution of 1956, which got rid of Rákosi. It lasted eleven days. The Russians suppressed it. '1968' means the 'Prague Spring', also suppressed, 1989 the fall of Communism in the Soviet Union and all its European satellites.

26
Hungary Hungary

How did the people live?
Misery misery.
How did the rulers live?
Tyranny tyranny.
What did the peasants think?
Apathy apathy.
What did the townsmen seek?
Livelihood livelihood.
What was the end of it?
Violence violence.

Did they begin again?
Painfully painfully.
What was the course they took?
Ruthlessness ruthlessness.
What was the aim of it?
Liberty liberty.
How did the country look?
Battlefields battlefields.
What was the name of it?
Hungary Hungary.

'Hungary Hungary' is partly an experiment in verse where the accent is predominantly on the first syllable, as is the way with the Hungarian language, giving it at times great power.

27
For the Common Market

It's easy to be witty in French,
You don't have to know French well –
Think of those French expressions (this is the secret):
Goût du néant, esprit de l'escalier,
Dégoût de la vie, nostalgie de la boue,
Adieu suprême des mouchoirs.
All you have to do is take two nouns,
Any old nouns, the iller-assorted the better,
And couple them with a genitive,
Shrug, throw your hands out (not too far)
In a French sort of way,
And give the casual knowing look of someone
Who knows the girl at the bar.

Try it and see...
With faint disdain...c'est un sentiment de vestiare,
Amour de boulanger, fantaisie du lavabo,
Goût de Londres, tendresse des wagon-lits;
Or, sighing,
Les au revoirs de Vendredi.
Everyone will say how well you know French.
I've tried it on Frenchmen and I know.

In German just couple the words together,
Like any old strangers meeting in any old street...
Himmelschnabel Heldenbegeisterung.Weltkrebs...
No one will know any better.

In Italian it will help to know the first lines of Dante;
And also, brushing away a tear,
Italia, Italia, terra di morti,
And go straight on to business.

I will advise later about the Scandinavian countries.

I wrote the above, light-heartedly, in the early days of what has now been for some time known as the European Community, to which Hungary now belongs. May they find lasting peace there, and may the Community benefit from a brilliant nation.

GROUP THREE

All these poems in Group Three have to do with Wales.

28
What I See

Vienna, yellow and green.
London, lavender.
Steel, for New York.
Beijing, a jewelled bird.
Urbino, white; Rome, golden.
Venice, a treasure raised.

And on these hills, this estuary,
Despair of painters, faithless,
Still difference in one place,
Still smiles, still sulks, still change,
A mood for every minute.
Stay for a picture, Wales!

Be something always!
Home of the looking-for-home.
Light like a pole-vaulter
Skims summits and is gone.
The diamond windows darken.
The raven clouds sail on.

29
Winter Viburnum

When the mountains wear white hoods, and furrows frost,
And the year is going to ground,
Thickets stripped of cover,
Gaitered and gunshot time, bad for the
Hungry, the homeless, and the hunted;

When the lake is a frozen ballroom, and round the ballroom
Trees like scrawny duennas
Spread naked fans,
That once so rustled and whispered, but now
Have nothing left but spokes;

There comes or, if come already, remains the tall
Hyacinth-scented, white,
Winter viburnum,
Flowering on the bare branch, in everything else
Belonging totally to spring.

Lovely indifference, so to continue playing,
When the orchestra's packed and gone,
The hall's unheated,
And those who assume a concert has come to an end,
When most of the instruments stop,

Long since withdrew to firesides, there to construct
Their antidotes to hope,
Expressing in brave
Bare lines the exquisite, unequivocal
Vacant finality of winter.

30
Beach Scene

Down this hot beach, with falcon eye,
The pioneers once sauntered by,
The poet-pirates,

And charmed ashore the siren girls
With crimson scarf, black grapes of curls,
And one gold earring.

Romance, romance, was rife that day.
The burghers locked their chests away.
And hid their daughters.

How Time has tamed those corsair looks!
O, the Long Johns, the Captain Hooks,
Who thumb the papers,

While stubby plump bedizened hands
Dispose the picnic on the sands...
The mermaid matrons.

Is it for joy from old times' sake
Some antique couples choose to take
Their Sunday outing

On what is now the Council's shore
To feel the ecstasy once more
In their inheritors?

And do they sense some sad remove
From that conquistadorial love,
Now it's gone public,

As home they stump to stoke the fire,
Still strong with mutual desire,
From days all wonder?

31
Mrs Williams Pugh

Garth Farm belonged to Mrs Williams Pugh
(Scottish by birth); most was only fit for a goat.
When I came back from the war and remarked on the view,
And she said, 'Yes, it makes one think
What the boys did for us',
Something caught in my throat.
She meant keeping the Nazis out. She'd have been a guerrilla,
Smuggling guns across mountains, caching dynamite
In baskets of eggs. They'd have had a job to kill her,
Sniping from rocks and digging pitfalls at night.

Her gods were God; on the human level,
The Queen; then 'the old gentleman' (Winston Churchill);
She considered Harold Wilson in league with the Devil,
And most of 'his lot' (Socialist
Squires and unsettled but wealthy settlers)
Certain of fire and brimstone.
'Them beauties' she called thinkers thronging valley and peak,
In fact all not living by hand or land,
Even Nobel prize-winners and Professors of Greek.
She should have had ten children and plenty of grand-

But had none. Her child was Bob Williams Pugh;
Retired from the quarries, a tiny bottle-shaped man,
Welsh to the roots, who knew little English, but knew
How to carve things in slate,

Such as a clover-leaf,
A prayer-book, a fan,
Or an inkstand, or a Lilliput furniture set.
He was always chuckling to himself. He left her a ring
And thirteen golden sovereigns. I shall never forget
The day he went, his sheepdog howling and howling.

She lived on alone.
We would have helped her to move, but she said she'd be lost,
The plains would have finished her. We put in a telephone,
Though she knew what went on
Without, through the postman, and hung up
In mid-speech because of the cost.
On she worked, dawn to dusk, then reading the Bible. The sole
  sign
Of something amiss was the cows went; then sheep; then bees;
  then
Mrs Williams Pugh. I see her still on the skyline,
Carrying our milk-can on the way to Heaven.

She was ceremonious. Didn't like to be kissed.
Too familiar. Whenever I tried,
She put up her crab-apple cheek as if at the dentist.
She loved my wife, and my wife
Loved her. They remained
Surnames till the day she died,
Though she signed herself 'Beatie', short for Beatrice.
I write, a bit late, as her Dante; and who knows? It might be
My epitaph that, for hers, I have written her this,
And that Mrs Williams Pugh, Garth Foel, put up with me.

The real name was Mrs Lloyd Williams, and her farm Garth Foel, Croesor. There is no reason to conceal her identity, and an abundance of good and happy ones to remember it. I had altered it for the sake of a rhyme.

32
A Nineteenth-Century Welsh Trial

It's a terrible case, Tom Ellis, Tom Ellis,
And judgment cannot be deferred.
Have you nothing to say not to put you away?
'He has nothing to say, my Lord.'

But did no one suggest it, Tom Ellis, Tom Ellis?
Did you act of your own accord?
We look kindly on crime when it's done the first time.
He answers, 'The Devil, my Lord.'

They say you read deeply, Tom Ellis, Tom Ellis,
In the hills, and revere the Good Word,
And the oath that you took with your hand on the Book.
He says yes, he reveres it, my Lord.

Then wherefore so silent, Tom Ellis, Tom Ellis?
And why no regrets to record?
No sign of repentance to mitigate sentence?
He says he's repented, my Lord.

But repentance so private, Tom Ellis, Tom Ellis,
Is repentance the laws disregard.
Let someone write down your reply to the Crown.
He says, 'It's all written, my Lord.'

Then let someone speak for you, Tom Ellis, Tom Ellis.
O, let somebody say a good word,
Some witness to honesty, decency, constancy.
He says 'There are plenty, my Lord.'

O, one is enough, Tom Ellis, Tom Ellis,
To enlighten the Court what occurred,
And tell us what led the accused to see red.
He says she can't come here, my Lord.

O no, she can't come here, Tom Ellis, Tom Ellis.
O never, to bed or to board.
And he's also in Hell, who's the cause that she fell.
And blood must have blood, saith the Lord.

33
Welsh Love Letter

Were all the peaks of Gwynedd
In one huge mountain piled,
Cnicht on Moelwyn,
Moel-y-Gest, Moel Hebog,
And Eryri on top,
And all between us,
I'd climb them climb them
All!
To reach you.
O, how I love you!

Were all the streams of Gwynedd
In one huge river joined,
Dwyfor, Dwyryd,
Glaslyn, Ogwen,
And Mawddach in flood,
I'd swim them swim them
All!
To reach you.
O, how I love you!

Were all the forts of Gwynedd
In one great fortress linked,
Caer and castle,
Cricieth, Harlech,
Conwy, Caernarfon,
And all in flames,
I'd jump them jump them
All!
To reach you.
O, how I love you!

See you Saturday,
If it's not raining.

Dannie Abse had encouraged and anthologised me some time ago, as did Dennis Enright, now dead, and I had been honoured and grateful to both. But I was amazed and overjoyed in 2003 to find myself in a new collection of Dannie's entitled Homage to Eros, *sub-titled* 100 Great Poems of Love and Lust, *with as book jacket a reproduction of Gustav Klimt's* The Kiss. *And there I was, in a Milky Way of lover-poets reaching from Song of Solomon, Catullus and Ovid, through Shakespeare, to, in our own day, Seamus Heaney, crowded with stars from many nations and centuries, at least twenty of first magnitude.*

The poem had come to me decades ago from a Welsh woman friend. At school her teacher of English used to have competitions in literary composition, mostly on usual subjects, but one in love-letters. The pattern depended on taking the mickey out of amorous young males, presumably Welsh. The girls had to think up the a few lines of bombast preceding the anti-climax of the last two. It was too good to miss. I think I wrote my three preceding verses almost at once. Revenue from the poem, anthologised many times, came as pennies from heaven on several occasions. Dannie, in his note introducing me, wrote that I was 'not averse to mocking my neighbours [i.e. Welsh] affectionately and comically'. True, but the idea originated with a Welsh woman, and those who most often quote the lines approvingly back to me are Welsh. I have tried (not very hard) to find a put-down so final, so brisk, so clinching, as part of the curriculum in English schools; so far in vain.

34
Spring Fever

Where has he got to? Missing from the Rotarians'
Dance for the District Nurse Fund, though he paid. Forcing
Excuses on a fistful of Committees,
And taking French
Leave from his roster on the Bench.
Inquiries sent in vain
From sports groups, teachers' outings, antiquarians,
And at the Annual General Meeting
Of the Glyndwr Club his empty chair again.

Where is our Iolo? Weeks now, and no one's seen
A sign of him. They ring and ring. No answer. Has he
Been ill, or absent? Absent, but not ill.
And now he's back in touch
From undivulged excursions, such
As make all Gwynedd say,
'How well he looks! Years younger. Has he been
To Tenby? Or perhaps the Costa Brava?'
No. Only a few miles. But every day.

35
End of a Summer Term

'TEACHERS WED': HEADLINE IN LOCAL NEWSPAPER

The chairs are piled. The Cambrian Snail,
Half London train, half dragon's tail,
Drops those who passed, or did not pass.
By tidal salting and shaven grass.
Goodbye reports, prizegiving days,
The all-too-hurried-explained
Rebukes, and never-questioned praise.
Goodbye the sweets and keepsakes rained
On favourite members of the staff,
And pleas for a last photograph.

The teachers' term ends too, to start
Their holidays abroad, apart.
Those goodbyes on the sands will do
Till autumn comes, to keep them true.
Symbols are always close at hand
In Wales: remembrances of sea,
That unclothes, then re-clothes the sand,
So peacefully, so constantly.
The estuaries are there to prove
That tides are metaphors for love.

Oh, will huge Elsewheres of Unrest,
Where landscapes face the market's test
And only rights to build excuse
These lonely lovely useless views,
Cry 'Home's a dustbin for the old.
Life, Life's for those who go away'?
Or will the ancient anchors hold,

And Coming-Back mean Come-to-Stay,
Mean Stay-for-Life, to reaffirm
The idyll of that summer term?

36
Turning Off

Bumper to bumper. Four miles from coast to church.
Constable Griffiths cut that snake in two
To admit a family in a family car.
Hoping to travel faster a longer way,
They had turned off yesterday on minor roads,
And become hysterical.

They had seen things.

They had met at twilight a defeated cortège,
Guarding a dying king in a tattered litter
To a shore where three queens waited.
When dark fell
A winged horse leaped from the mountains
And left, wherever he touched, horseshoes of light
That disappeared in a lake. At midnight
A sword waved from the lake's blackness, and seven swans
Sailed past, wearing coronets.
A courier bent low and shouted something.
The air was torn with cries.
In the small hours' silence
They had heard the rocks pushing, the slow shoving
In earth's night, the slip, the slide, and the inrush
Of oceans, and wind slicing the summits;
And had seen the crystals that glittered as they formed

Round the dead gossiping in crevices five hundred
Million years before Christ, and an old lady
In her winding-sheet, muttering as in life;
While those for whom the willow weeps in slate
Whistled in the deep dark veins
Under the chert and quartz.
Dawn had brought ghosts of the sea
Streaming along the saltings, then farm after farm
Took off like seagulls into a thunder sky.
But when sun rose
Apples were golden in cottage gardens
And fleeces touched with gold.

'You saw all that?'
'Yes...yes!'
'O, but we never bother with it',
So, some inhabitants; or else,
'We seldom see it now.'

The strangers are reassured.
It had seemed so clear something was about to be born.
But unprepared
By any hint in the weather report or guide-book,
This turning-off had made them at first uneasy,
Then afraid, then so nearly mad,
They felt it a kind of bliss to be reincorporated
Into the snake again, embedded fore and aft
In the familiar nuisances.

You could have seen them later,
Picnicking a couple of yards from the road,
Perfectly self-possessed.

37
Property

'Ten, fifty thousand would not be too much.
This field would fetch a really princely sum.
Developers would give their eyes for such
A view as this. Both sea and mountains!'

Or so he said. And nothing answered she,
Trailing in tall wild weeds a small white hand,
Thinking the view seemed risen from the sea,
Like painted meadows in a Book of Hours.

38
Olwen Pugh

We are back as before, less one. Six farmers home.
The Reverend Griff takes choir practice. At the Plas,
Now flats, our sage is taking
A walk round his doubts. Inigo, sculptor and letterer,
Takes measurements, happy with slate. And close
(We are a community)
Lived Olwen Pugh, who took an overdose.

She never attended at church, but Inigo
Found a spare headstone. Our sage, for whom once she
did,
Said something beautiful.
The Reverend Griff registered her. Four of the farmers
Lowered bitter old Olwen into her slot

As first-class mail, and the view
Lived up to its reputation as a beauty spot.

And all night long she has crouched among my words
With one shoe off, shuffling and turning them over,
Muttering about wanting
More than mere burial. 'What do you mean... "more"'? No one
Trespassed on your lunacy, Olwen Pugh.
And if 'more' means 'haunting',
Something happened to ghosts, and nothing happened to you.

39
Twm Williams

He used to stand at the crossroads,
Beetle-browed like an admiral.
When visitors asked, 'Can you tell
Us the way to the hotel?'
(It had a name for adul-
-tery, and other deeds extra-marital),
He would gaze at the chauffeur, the seal-
-skin car, the model,
Her sleek cavalier, and the beautiful
Leather valises, each label
From this or that or the other swell
Spa, their *je ne sais quel*
Air of things Continental,
And in tones like a funeral knell
Reply, 'A very long way from God.'

Last of the prophets, old bard,
Toothed on the Gospel,
Jeremiah Isaiah Ezekiel,
Twice on Sundays plus Sunday school,
Twm Williams, an old-style Wel-
-shman...but the *hwyl*.
The *hwyl* is gone from the Chapel.
No more the petrified thrill,
As the minister in the pul-
-pit draws his bow, and the people
Divide for the arrow to fall,
'Not on me, O Almighty!' Now all
Expect Heaven of right, and Hell
Is a difficult plot to sell.
Twm Williams takes it ill
That so few repair to the Lord.

I said to him once at the crossroad
(Grey mane, a gash by each nostril),
'Do you recall, Twm Will-
-iams, that time in the war, when to muddle
Any impudent Nazi devil,
Dropped by river or fell,
Or sneaking down from the Wirral,
Or across the Cambrian Channel,
Not a signpost was left to reveal
One place-name, no maps were for sale,
Direction was undesirable?'
And gravely from under his beetle
Brows came back, 'I've no need to recall.
There is no direction still.
The signposts were never restored.'

40
A Last Mention

Places I haven't written about,
A mention now. Forgive
That no rhyme came,
Though not for want of thought,
For you especially,
Quarry, gashed, gaunt,
Silver against black mountains,
Or black against white clouds, where daily I've
Imagined names of the immortals carved;
Beeches and sycamores, so brilliant-green,
With shadows between, raven as Welshmen's hair;
Small birds, feeding in such fear
They must get ulcers; owl,
Hooting whenever a plank of light from the door
Falls by his tree; absolving
Waters between whom and hills
Dangles this Ithaca of ours; and every
Till now protector, how or wheresoever,
Or riding on or rising from the sea, or
Wind-blown from past knowing; all
Who came, will come, us here, us one day gone;
Farms, meadows, roses;
A people garrulous, withdrawn,
And quiet as this house,
As this page closes.

41
Millennium

Slow from the sea the great seculars moved to the birth, on waves
collapsed with their weight of fame.
The religious too were arriving, as mountains seem to move
when really it is the clouds.
The flambeau'd apostles stood looking after their master,
for whom the last step had been flight.
The old gods lolled on the clouds as if at a *fête champêtre*.
Angels reclined along branches.
Sun streamed between the aged, so heavy with their wisdom,
one wondered how they had got there,
As one wonders about Stonehenge, whom the sun
also streams through; and the sailors
Swept in from oceans, dressed-ship from the funeral they'd given
to the last nuclear weapon.

It was not a formal occasion. No one on balconies.
Nowhere would have been long enough
For all with a right to appear, who had died and suffered,
the named, the numberless nameless.
No music was played, no speeches given. It just came about.
People just found themselves there,
Gossiping in amazement of the times that had gone before.
Was it possible? Could such things
Truly have happened? Did we really talk in that way
(Pre-emptive strikes, and so on)?

All this befell to celebrate the first child born
after those arms were abolished,
Some time about the first day of the first month in the year…
I forget; except

It was something to have happened to be there,
    though now it's absorbed, we're peaceful.
As we should have been, when the great names said their sayings
    and the apostles stood staring
At their various masters vanishing various ways.
    It was something, yes, to have been there
To hear, stronger than trumpets, the hush, and feel on our cheeks
    that breeze, as it might have been Paradise.

I remember, going away, how the poets asked one another,
    'Now that those horrors are done with,
How shall we manage without fear, and the ancient tensions?
    How can there ever be poets
After this? Poets are not all that accustomed to joy. Of course
    the earth will be here,
The tumultuous oceans, birds, the beasts in the fields,
    sun, moon, stars, all that,
But so many have written of them. This is
    a new situation.'

Oh well, we decided, Death will remain, and the unfortunate
    will want visions of Hereafter.
And if the fortunate rampage on to unbelievable ages,
    the sadder they'll be to go.
And countries will stop having anthems with much
    about conquests, but instead
About bards, and fierce conversation. About almost
    anything. But especially
Bards. And there will always be Wales, and in Wales
    We shall still have our vocation.

GROUP FOUR

Lit Crit

I have given this group a frivolous title, partly because I have read far too little poetry, in English or any other language, to stake any claim in the fields of literary criticism. Poems 42–50 are random instinctive reactions to certain lines of criticism by others. It gave me a lot of pleasure to invent the publishing firm of Pfirtzhiemer and Kramp. They happen to be American, but might exist and flourish in many countries, the UK not least. Of the remainder, may I suggest to other would-be poets that, if short of inspiration and not already aware, an almost inexhaustible gold-mine awaits them among characters in the Bible and the plays of Shakespeare. The last two poems can be taken as self-criticism.

42
Critic on Poet

He wrote some verse one might call good.
But all the rest one understood.

43
A Disappointment

Mr Pfirtzhiemer was disappointed in this author.
I too. We'd been so sure. Mr Pfirtzhiemer ordered
A farm in New Hampshire, and Mrs Kramp and I
Reserved for a summer in Venice. This author seemed
Possessed, shall I say, of a sensitivity

Uncommon today, a freshness. He lived in the country.
When he came to town he called it 'a huge bazaar,
Like Constantinople'. No one had ever said that;
Or not in our hearing. We saw ourselves on cushions,
Doing something with sherbet. In the outer office
Miss Jackson's eyes turned almond, and all Manhattan
Withdrew behind a yashmak.
We have a superior line, but we were waiting.
This must be the promised one.

He began with a project about Emily Dickinson.
She was, as he termed it, just making the swing-doors.
The draft had a tenderness, a kind of sort of
Adamant tenderness (he named it so himself).
By the time he had finished, Emily Dickinson
Was out on the sidewalk again. His next, an elegy,
Was moving about Grant's Tomb. It took three years.
I won't trouble you with the rest, except to say
He possessed that gift, amounting almost to genius,
Of knowing when the wind of favour would veer,
And of getting his sails up just in the nick of time
To see it veer back again. Everything he composed
Gleamed with that youthfulness very rare in our day.
If we detected sometimes a trace of flatness,
He assured us it was deliberate. He taught us much
About the power of the monosyllable to depress.
Thinking about it, I could not have faced the subway,
Had it not been for the lift of the long 'u's,
Elided 'i's and agitation of female endings.
Vowels, he said, were flowers, consonants railroads
(T's going west, M's east). Punctuation, he said,
Is a poet's Morse. We thought that beautiful.
He was great on assonance. It was great to be taking around
A man in whom you could *sense* the internal rhymes.
We wished only that speech, when it came, fell faster
On to the page. His lines on Paul Valéry in Harlem...

There were only two…took a year. His first wife
Walked out after his first lyric, and he withdrew it.
We tried to understand, though once he told us
That a poet's pen is dipped in his tears (a sentiment
Later transferred to rhyme)…

There were no hard feelings.

He kept to the end that unpolluted quality.
After the advance he never spoke about money.
We did not ask it back, having ourselves been touched
By something of his spiritual deodorant,
If I may put it so, as indeed he put it.

He died while still composing his own epitaph.
Now we no longer take foghorns for the muezzin.
Miss Jackson's eyes have gone back to blackcurrant.
And by the time we get something from the afterworld,
I fear that religious belief will be out again.
In due course a memoir will be in the bookshops,
Though not published by Pfirtzhiemer and Kramp.
H used to say one should not be subject to fashion,
But one has to live. Pfirtzhiemer has no country home.
Mrs Kramp and I are spending the summer in Brooklyn,

Richard Hughes, author of A High Wind in Jamaica *and other famous works, our friend and neighbour, remarked after he read this poem that it was an exact description of himself. The remark had a posthumous sadness. He referred to the writing of his trilogy which begins with* The Fox in the Attic *as 'a race with the undertaker' and died before he could finish it.*

44
More from the Files

I

Here's a much simpler one, right out of the top of the bag.
He writes two novels a year. After the first success
He never took one step forwards. All the advances are made
By Pfirtzhiemer and Kramp, and get bigger and bigger
As we cover the one before. We like to call him
'Favourite of the Muses', meaning Emily Pfirtzhiemer
Who thanks to him found her husband easier to live with,
And my own Cornelia Kramp, whom thanks to him
I was able to deck with gems and take to New Mexico.
And of such is the Kingdom of Heaven, though I hope not yet.

2

I, Ed Kramp, found this one. Another poet. Difficult
At a quick glance, but so have they all been. I sent his first
Collection to Hiram Whitaker, whose critical perceptions
(Published by Pfirtzhiemer and Kramp) have introduced so many
Young champions into, as I call it, the ring of literature.
He picked one poem especially, which runs as follows,
With Hiram's comments beneath. The poet had called it

'Sehnsucht'

> Unto what anthracite masks
> Mount, O Aloha,
> The oars of your million guitars?
> And on what a unicorn,
> Stucco, with castor feet,
> Gloriana, you come, you come!
> Long have I waited with my rolled umbrella,

My shoe-sad feet burning the pavement,
Mercury, for your wings;
Remembering Athens and the stale tobacco,
My mother's hand in my hair and the wild cuckoo,
In this house of sad shoes and sorrow and stucco,
And Rome, ah Rome!
E pericoloso sporgersi.

'Why, this is masterly!' (Hiram replied).
'Observe the juxtaposition in the first six lines –
The old romantic symbols, with their loitering sounds
('Aloha', 'unicorn', 'Gloriana'), and the brisk syllables
Of the humdrum ('stucco' repeated); then in line seven;
Reminiscence of Eliot, but absorbed completely;
  counterpoise
'Shoe-sad' against 'Mercury', who of course wore no shoes.
Reprise next of the classical age ('ah, Rome!'), accepted
As having no further validity; then ...this bit is perfect...
His mother's hand not 'on', but 'in' his hair, recalling –
Rimbaud? The earlier Lafargue? And that exquisite coda,
The notice in Italian railway carriages:
'It's dangerous to lean out.'

This is your man, Ed Kramp.
As for technique, his manoeuvring of the vowels
Is such, as it were, almost to liquefy the consonants,
So that the total effect, while remaining dense, becomes fluvial.
Rhythm and content? Assured. He can do it all on his head.
Some may say that he has. I'll help you to deal with them.
He's clearly holding back, afraid to stick his neck out;
'Long have I waited'...Let him wait no longer. Publish him.

So we did. Or I did. Pfirtzhiemer was against. I took
The remaindered copies home. 'Don't worry,' Mrs Kramp said.
'We only hear of Daniel's successes. We never hear about
The prophecies he got wrong.' We stored the books in the cellar,

An investment for our grandchildren, Sharon and Edgar Allan.
We check them for damp (the books). When Hiram comes to
dinner –
Less often now than before – we read passages aloud to him.

45
The Spider in the Bath

We (Pfirtzhiemer and Kramp) used to send you bulletins,
Through our London agents, about the State of Poetry.
In this new issue I present an Aesthetic Dilemma
('I' am Ed Kramp. Mr Pfirtzhiemer missed Aesthetics)
Confronting, and soon to be solved by Hiram Whitaker,
Whose critical writings (published by Pfirtzhiemer and Kramp)
Are required reading in schools and prisoners' courses
And on ten-year discount to old-age pensioners.

Mr Whitaker had been awarded the Howitzer Medal
For his brilliant, definitive and seminal work
On the poet X. It illumined from the one word 'Now',
In X's famous line 'My God is Now',
X's ideological U-turn. Hiram (we have him to dinner)
Had also turned (as I call it) the searchlight of analysis
On X's manipulation of rhythm, with particular reference
In Chapter Five to his post-Freudian use of the anapaest.
All this was going ahead in thousands of copies, when X,
Whom many thought dead, announced that he scanned as two
Beats what Hiram had scanned as one, and 'put in a lot'
(So he claimed) 'because it just sounded right'. He also
Revealed that 'Now' had been a printer's error for 'Not'.

So Hiram is busy now on a book, *The Spider in the Bath*.
The Spider stands for poets who foolishly emerge

Into the cold enamel sheen of criticism (the Bath).
When a hand (Hiram) reaches down that's trying to help them
Away from wrong directions, they scuttle, shed legs,
Anything rather than being put back
In the plug-hole's 'creative darkness' (a classic phrase).
Criticism and comments on criticism, as Hiram makes clear,
Are not their habitat, as the Bath is not the Spider's.

X, rather peevishly, has refused a preface; although doubtless
The book might bolster his sales (we do not publish him),
And involve quite a number of analytical teenagers,
Prisoners, and old-age pensioners with nothing better to do.

46
To a Forced Voice

It is not enough to write elegies to tractors,
If you return each evening and hang your hat
In the neat white cloakroom of your neat white flat.

It is not enough to blast the people to battle,
If you have never had part in a battle yourself.
It is not enough to take from the dustered shelf

The anger of others and bottle it as your own,
And chatter like parrot or monkey of golden dawns.
You are following feet that have walked on the world's thorns,

And if your heart has never worn ragged clothes,
And if it has never been wounded, whatever the pain,
All you can shout of the sorrows of others is vain.

47
The Owl

There was an old owl that lived in a wood.
He worried as much as worry he could,
And the more he found
About terrible things that went on above ground,
His head grew hot and his eyes grew round,
And the more, the more,
The more he stared at what happened there,
The more, the more he worried.

He called his brother and sister owls,
And said 'Since we are the wisest fowls,
We must start some schools
For all these trivial feckless fools,
And have more meetings, and make more rules,
And end the singing, their singing.
An end, an end.
The linnet we'll tell, and the lark as well,
The time for songs is finished.'

So all the wood was as quiet as death.
Any bird that sang, even under its breath,
Was chained on sight,
And judged by the owls sitting day and night,
And hung in a cage without any light;
And the owls they governed, they governed,
So stern, so stern,
They cured the wood of its frivolous mood,
And put an end to the singing.

They dug some ditches and laid some paths,
And gave some lectures and built some baths,
And covered the trees
With useful mottoes and wise decrees
For putting out fires and curing disease,
Till the wood was grateful, grateful.
And yet, and yet,
The groves seemed dead, since the music had fled,
And no one was contented.

And a whisper ran through the branches green
That the ban on ballads would never have been,
If the owls could sing,
For this, it was said, was the only thing
That they could not do, and that was the sting.
And it happens, yes, it happens,
Owls or men, owls or men,
Get their own back for the spirit they lack
By banning it in others.

The whisper spread till the chief owl heard.
He called all the owls, did that stately bird,
To his treetop throne,
Where he sat in the ring of the moon alone,
And he said 'Our voices are very well known.
If you doubt it, follow, just follow.'
And they did, they did,
As he cleared his throat and gave them a note,
They followed him in the chorus.

And the moment their eerie shanty began,
From burrow and branch the little birds ran.
They had nothing to say,
But they laughed all night and they laughed all day,
Till they almost laughed their feathers away.
They'd seen nothing like it, like it,

And the owls, the owls,
They jumped and shrieked till the whole wood creaked,
But no one could call it singing.

And that was the end of the ban on song.
After the laughter it couldn't last long.
And the owls, they swore
To study in secret, but never learned more
Than humming the Dead March in front of a score.
And the moral is, the moral,
Far better, far,
That the owl should hum than the lark be dumb,
Or the nightingale turn solemn.

Wishful thinking. I wish its message could be true to what usually happens. It is true that dictators are frightened of poets, since what poets write of them is often damning and survives them; but they do not try to write poetry themselves. They try to destroy the poets. In my lifetime, in the Soviet Union, Osip Mandelstam was dispatched to certain death; Pasternak was 'only' prevented from receiving the Nobel Prize; Anna Akhmatova, thank God, survived in Russia to write superb poetry, but had suffered too much, unlike the little birds in the poem, to make fun of owls. In Spain Lorca was brutally murdered by Franco's Fascists. For my owl I was thinking especially of Stalin. There was something almost rounded, completely cosmically icy about his cruelty that might have fitted into the 'ring of the moon'; and at least he had rather a grand eclipse. Hitler was altogether too messy and too commonplace.

48
Getting Distanced

I should like to tell you more about Pfirtzhiemer and Kramp,
Our publishing firm in Manhattan. I've sent you bulletins
Through our London agents about one of our Disappoint-
ments
(See Chatto and Windus, *Out on a Limb*, page nine, one
pound),
Now I would like to consider another poet,
Whom we did rather better with, although (we accept this)
Less *succès fou* than *d'estime*. The thing about this one
Was that he had a thing. He was identifiable.
What he said was this: a poet has got to get distanced.
His personal life doesn't matter. The only matter that matters
Is his work, brothers, his work. Like William Shakespeare, I
said,
In his Sonnets (Mr Pfirtzhiemer hasn't read them.
Mr Pfirtzhiemer, between you and me, is rather a Philistine).
To which this artist replied: 'Shakespeare so distanced himself
That even today professors at Harvard and Princeton
Can't say for sure who he was.' Mr Pfirtzhiemer understood
distance.
Not intellectually (between you and me and in confidence
He has no intellect); but for many years he'd been distanced
From Mrs Pfirtzhiemer. They occupied separate apartments
(Charged to the firm). I tried to organise distance
From Mrs Kramp, but no go. Somehow it wouldn't work.
'Ed,' she would say, 'Ed Kramp, what on earth's come over
you?
You seem so far away.' And the more she said it, the closer
I seemed to get to her. This is personal and irrelevant.
I'm talking about this poet. It used to astonish us,

The way he distanced himself from previous wives and lovers.
Though you always knew who it was. That was his
Identifiable thing. He had a powerful influence
On many, including me, Ed Kramp – not as a publisher,
But as a human being – not that the difference matters,
Though one has to live. I'm beginning to lose the thread
Of what I was trying to tell you, and anyhow
It's all in his published works, which we dazedly published,
And those early revealing letters he wanted destroyed,
But his friends kept selling, to help in these difficult times.

49
In Japan

In Japan the poets write to each other
'I wish I could write like you.
I go on dabbing at screens with my tired brushwork.
Yours is so brave and new.'

In Japan the poets reply to each other:
'The first polish of words is mine,
Which produces a mist. The second (Esteemed Sir)
Is yours, which makes them shine.'

In Japan the poets cable the critics:
'Disgusted at line you took
About my latest stop how dare honoured Sir
Recommend so worthless book.'

In Japan the poets write to the editors:
'Thanks for returning enclosure
To this insignificant person, thereby
Saving him public exposure.'

In Japan the poets say to the public:
'Thank you for being immense.
I refund in part for poems that have no rhythm;
In full if they have no sense.'

And publishers receive verses
In paint on a faded fan:
'This humble singer rejoices in those you left out.'
That's how it is in Japan.

A friend of mine told me she did not understand this poem and showed it to a Japanese scholar, who said that Japan is not at all like that. Later she showed it to her sister, who explained that I had not meant Japan to be really like that, but thought I was paying the Japanese a compliment in imagining that it is, as Great Britain is not.

50
On the Death of Mrs Kramp

I have tried to keep personalities out of these bulletins,
Bearing in mind that writers and, even more, publishers
Must distance themselves; but felt certain you would not object
If now in this issue I refer to my wife Cornelia,
Who died in April; a woman born straight from a furnace;
Née Fischbein (to be exact), half Jewish and half Quaker,
From Philadelphia; a woman no one could call beautiful;
Jolie laide is the French term; I thought her Assyrian-looking,
Until she asked me if I'd ever seen an Assyrian,
And likened her mouth to the Gulf of Mexico, her chin to Cape Cod.
She had a violent side. It expressed itself in her jewellery.

Which always seemed about to explode: dynamite round her neck,
Tenderness in her hands; a woman who got away with things...
She punctured attitudes; and when told of Q (very famous)
That his verse improved as he compressed it, she dared the reply
That for her it would reach its peak when it vanished completely.
She would never have said that of anyone struggling. Some of you
Owed your names to her at the start. First she won me over,
Then she went on at Pfirtzhiemer; and if he wouldn't yield,
She paid publication herself out of the housekeeping money
In our early days, when the Fischbeins docked her allowance
For marrying me, Ed Kramp. She was difficult to upset.
When Mr Ginsburg removed his pants at one of her parties,
She took them upstairs and ironed them. O, those parties, those
parties!
'You must understand' she told me 'that certain folk won't come
If So-and-So is coming, and others won't come if he isn't.
Make them all come, and get into each other. Our job's
To take care of the drink, and if the Pfirtzhiemers have to be
asked,
See they leave early.' O my, those parties! One of you said
The Renaissance had ceased to be the Duchess of Somewhere or
Other
At her great window in the dawn, and become Cornelia Kramp
Broaching a case of Bourbon. One dawn, when you'd all seeped
home,
I found her reading. 'What are you reading?' 'I am reading', she
said,
'About two of our guests where this critic says that that poet
Reflects the rhythms of ordinary speech. These are the poems, and
Ed Kramp,' she said, 'no ordinary speech that ever came my way
Rhythmed like this. It's eyewash.' Z...one of you...loved her.
Don't think I don't know. She said the world would be changed,
When writers make epigrams about virtues instead of vices.
All this will be forgotten. I shall never forget.
But I and her children will die, and then it will be forgotten.
She left a letter behind. It said:

'I bequeath certain memories to Z, to use as mythology;
My carcase, if they'll have it, to the Museum of Modern Art;
And my heart to my husband, who has had it for forty years.'
Remember her in, or whatever their substitute is, your prayers.

51

Easter Saturday and The Merchant of Venice

He must have heard as a boy,
When, certainly, whatever else is uncertain,
He went to church, the reiterated
'Haec est nox' in the liturgy;
'This is the night' in the Easter liturgy,

With its recital of ancient nocturnal
Rescuings by Yahweh of his chosen people.
And though in the Warwickshire summer a wasp
Or a face may have kept his thoughts
From perfect attention, the cadence stayed in his mind.

Till, years later, possibly needing a love-scene
To lighten the end of a play,
Even harder for us today,
The beautiful rhythm returned and he echoed it,
Writing, 'In such a night
Stood Dido...young Lorenzo...
Pretty Jessica...
In such a night....'
In such a night.

52
Malvolio's Revenge

SHAKESPEARE 1600 – JUGOSLAVIA 1946

The sensual shade of cypress and campanile
Lengthens across the terrace; above the sea
Argosies of a long Dalmatian evening
Set towards Venice; lutes accompany
The oleander and the olive tree,
Burning beyond the dancers. There are three
Couples: Viola and the Duke; Olivia
And Sebastian; Maria and Sir Toby.
The lizard pants on the sepia wall. Green shutters,
Like vertical eyelids, open on rooms of cool
Alabaster, tapestries, gardens, fountains.
The dance beginning now will be danced again...

Will be danced through Time, through Time,
That tall black frantic torn clocktower of a man
Suddenly strikes his horrifying chime:
'I'll be revenged on the whole pack of you!'
Why don't they freeze? Whenever I hear that line,
Someone is showing me my grave.

Olivia runs after him. Too late.
He has gone to his garret of Bibles and pomades,
There in hot tears to empty
Himself of delicacy for ever
And vow his passion to a different fever,
While they dance on, dance on...

With Time that dances, runs, meanders;
Three and a half centuries later

Brings us again to Ragusa golden
In the blue hair of the Adriatic,
Same palace, terrace, all
Save Olivia
Killed, refugee, arrested, all save she
Detained in her own house, thinking:

'Who is this captor-captain,
Grey-tunicked puritan-partisan, to me
So uncommonly courteous?'

'You gave me this,' he says.
Something from innocence, from long ago.
'Malvolio!'

'Yes, changed.
Prison and insult, branding...

Pilloried in the camp,
Feet half-lifted, all day on the parade-ground,
Tyrannies seen I had not known existed,
Led by my own wrong to the wrongs of others,
Led by my own lack to the lacks of others,
Mocked and not having you
Kindred to Cyrano, Quasímodo,
Jew Süss, Till Eulenspiegel, Heathcliff,
I fought for them. You only
Once moved towards me in compassion, once
Held out your hand. I love you.'

Only on her he will not take revenge.
Lets her escape...a secret stair?
A submarine? In exile
To smell, or think she smells the linden tree,
See something like an oleander, but not quite,
Come on some heartache view, start suddenly crying...
Who knows?

At Windsor in the Second Folio,
A delicate hand scores out on the title-page
'Twelfth Night', and writes 'Malvolio'.
Perhaps King Charles heard
As I, whenever I hear that line, hear muskets,
See war,
See civil war,
And some long-afterwards
Olivia and Malvolio,
Illyria again.

After the war I went to Jugoslavia for The Times, *first to report the trial in Belgrade of General Draza Mihailovich, leader of the Chetniks, whom Communist Marshal Tito and his partisans had defeated in the civil war they had waged against one another, concurrently with the part both had played in the World War against the Nazis. The next occasion was a year later when, as resident correspondent in Hungary 'with responsibility for the Balkans', I had settled down with Mary on Gizi Bajor's top floor in Budapest. Within days came the world-astounding news that Tito, hitherto thought of as being on the best of terms with the Soviet Union, had had a row with Stalin and been expelled from the Cominform, which meant of course, among his vassal countries, Hungary.*

We went to Jugoslavia as soon as we could get permits in Budapest (not easy; we were now, as regards communications, on a second tightrope, the other being between Stalinist Hungary and bourgeois-democratic Vienna in the West). At the time this split behind the Iron Curtain was a very big story indeed. I sent many messages from Jugoslavia and paid visits to several regions. One journey took us to Dalmatia on the Adriatic coast. We had rooms in a hotel in Dubrovnik (Ragusa, its old name, in the poem), where for a moment I ceased to be a journalist and said to Mary, 'Now we are in Shakespeare' i.e. the seacoast in Illyria, the old name for part of Dalmatia, where he opens the second scene of Twelfth Night. *I* thought of Viola, often played by Viola Tree, to whom her father gave the name. And of Malvolio. But the poem had to wait seventeen years.

In 1966 I had an invitation from McMaster University, Ontario, to give two talks at a Shakespeare seminar that summer. It came thanks to Michael Langham, who had directed two plays of mine in England and was now in charge of the Shakespeare Memorial Theatre in Stratford, Ontario. I told Bertrand Russell that the prospect scared me a little, since nearly all the other speakers would be professors with an intimate knowledge of Shakespeare I lacked. I would have accepted anyhow, since Mary was invited with me, and his reply, 'They're all scoundrels', reassured me. I decided on two titles: the first, 'Why No Henry VII?', to be followed by 'Malvolio's Revenge', and spent many weeks preparing them. They went down well. I was asked to repeat them and allowed to defer one repetition in order, on television, to watch England defeat Germany at football in the final of the World Cup. McMaster published the first talk and an abridgment of the second, together with all the others by the experts. I need not trouble readers with anything about the first, since I have no poem on which to hang it.

To me Malvolio is one of the great Mocked-at Upstarts in literature; and Olivia is genuinely attached to him. I love *Twelfth Night*, even at times his persecutors, even the drunken sponger Sir Toby Belch. Mary did not much care for it, despite Viola and so many imperishable passages. She did not like to witness the mocking of any human being, whatever the provocation. When my first dispatches about the Mihailovich trial appeared in *The Times*, she wrote from London: 'I find the trial disturbing to my sense of justice. Your reporting is extremely good, but you too give the impression that you are infected by a certain inhumanity of the mass against a man reduced to an indignity.' She was reconciled by my record of his last words, translated innocently by my Serbo-Croat interpreter into such rare and perfect English, and often quoted: 'Fate was merciless when it threw me into this maelstrom. I wanted much, I started much, but the gale of the world carried away me and my work.'

I saw Malvolio as a Puritan, and his persecutors in the light in which Lucy Hutchinson, one of the bravest and most lovable Puritans, saw the cheap mockery Puritanism had to endure: 'All that crossed the views of the needy courtiers,' she wrote in her Life *of her Puritan soldier-husband, 'all who could not endure blasphemous oaths, ribald conversation, profane scoffs...all these were Puritans...branded beside as illiterate, morose, melancholy, discontented, crazed sort of men...as such they were made the sport ...of every stage, and every table and puppet-play* belched *[my underlining] forth against them, the drunkards made them their songs.....' Surely she must have seen the play and, with indignation and disgust, registered Sir Toby.*

I long to see a production – and there may have been many, since it is seldom off some stage somewhere – in which Malvolio is shown handsome enough to justify the vanity that makes him hope Olivia may fall in love, requite the love of a desperately lonely man and help him with a career of which he knows himself to be capable. The lines are there to show that she has high regard for his ability and honesty, and that Maria, Olivia's handmaid, is jealous of his standing with her. I see him as a forefather of all who have risen from poverty to power, like some of Tito's partisans, accounts of whom, brought back to Churchill, helped to persuade him to drop Mihailovich and support Tito. The final scene should be immensely powerful. Malvolio, insulted, dishevelled, ridiculous, can still have dignity with his first line, addressed to Olivia as if his contemptible tormentors were not even there:

Madam, you have done me wrong,
Notorious wrong.

And she, as soon as she understands the trick they have played on him in her name, promises him

This practice hath most shrewdly passed upon thee;
But when we know the grounds and authors of it,
Thou shalt be both the plaintiff and the judge
Of thine own cause.

Her next line, 'Alas, poor fool, how have they baffled thee!', should have the beginnings of shame and anger against the ganging-up.

'And', I ended my talk, 'as the "poor fool" thunders out his final exit line, one of the most bitter, powerful and prophetic threats in the whole of Shakespeare, 'I'll be revenged on the whole pack of you', a moment's silence should fall and we should hear (offstage) the muskets. Twelfth Night *was Shakespeare's "farewell to mirth". Ahead, in the life of his imaginings, wait* Hamlet, Othello, Macbeth, Lear; *in real life, though not his own, waited the Civil War, Malvolio's revenge.'*

53
Hamlet, *Act Three Scene Two*

End of the Players' scene.
The Players bow. The Court
Wait for a hint what sort
Of hand to give; and, 'Very nice, we thought.
Nice evening,' says the King.
'Riveting, darling Hamlet,' says the Queen.
Today that's how it would have been.

No guilt. No horror-strike. No fuss.
What follows: 'Lights, away!'
Just business for a play,
Which we, who watch our murders every day,
Applaud as thrilling and ingenious,
But false to Life. Especially to us.

54
If I Have a Fault

'If I have a fault,' he exclaims, and you think he'll own
He's a thief, or a forger of contracts.
Instead he declares a disastrous craving to give.
'Any rogue in a fix can count on me for a loan.
I'm too impulsive.'

'If I have a fault,' she begins, and you think she'll end
With possessiveness, or a mania
For mailing anonymous libels. Instead she berates
Herself for being too open, 'simply cannot pretend'
To like people she hates.

'If we have a fault,' they confide, and you wait to share
Admissions of cruelty, spite, betrayal. Instead they sigh
'How lazy we are. Insulted, how little we care.
How ineptly we lie.'

Endearing foibles, even foibles in virtues' dress,
They will grant, never anything nasty.
Hypocrite birds! What fun to put salt
On their tails! A weakness I have to confess,
If I have a fault...

55
The Telephone Clock

If days without praise ever chanced to extend,
He dialled the telephone clock
Just as a minute was ready to end,
And said,
'No one living or dead
Has ever been nicer or more self-effacing than me,
And not many more gifted.'
The receiver was ready to hand.
He had only to lift it
And a lacquered voice came through
With the answer he deemed his due.
He got to timing it perfectly.

A curse on the person he took for a friend:
He said 'Check the time for me, cock,'
And just as the minute was ready to end,
That snake
Gave him the phone and remarked,
'You take the cake
As one of the vainest men there can be.
Of the bogus élite
You are the monumentallest. Your core of conceit
Swells inversely with your skill,
Which very soon now will be nil.'
And the lacquered voice said, 'Precisely.'

GROUP FIVE

Farewells

The poems in this Group are in memory of people now dead: some famous, some friends, among them my friends killed at St Nazaire and those who have died since, one young and martyred, and the scrapman, an entertaining rogue.

56
Two Epitaphs

1
FOR ANDRÉ GIDE

Çi-Gide

2
FOR KARL MARX

Hairy, hairy, still contrary,
Next in the dictionary
To the Virgin Mary.

57
In Memory of Bahram Dehqani-Tafti

MURDERED IN IRAN MAY 1980,
AGED TWENTY-FOUR

One winter's night, says a cathedral booklet,
A mason hung his slate out, and it rained,
And down the slate the rain froze, perpendicular.
And in the morning the new style was born.

Tears ought to freeze into some architecture
Of words for Bahram slain. Words ought to soar
Into some west window of an ode; not shrink,
Equivocate, the Poets being embarrassed.

The Poets grant, knowing he was a Christian:
'O yes, a brave life...even beautiful...
Martyred for Human Rights...' and that will do.
Crucifixion they can take; not Resurrection.

Not 'Faith was part of him, and those who loved him.
And God has put his faithful through the fire,
Working through suffering; and will not fail
To reunite them, and forgive his murderers.'

I never learned the language you returned to,
Nor knew the country you refused to flee.
To me it just meant poverty, and domes, and princes
Sauntering through gardens among nightingales.

The East my boy's imagination fed on
I never dreamed would disquiet me with this death,
Or show me Oxford's happy scholar lying
Like a young saint in jewelled Isfahan.

Bahram was an Iranian Christian. His father was Anglican Bishop in Iran when the revolution against the Shah and Western influence broke out; he and his wife had reluctantly to flee for their lives to England, where he was given the bishopric of Basingstoke in honour and for livelihood. Bahram was a brilliant scholar-musician at Jesus College, Oxford, with a promising future in the West. Very courageously he decided it his duty to return to Iran; Moslem extremists murdered him. I said this poem at a service for prisoners of conscience in the chapter-house of Westminster Abbey; and again at the memorial service for Bahram in Jesus College Chapel, when some of his music was played. To my regret, I never met him.

58
Churchill

I spent the night on the pavement for Churchill's funeral.
It was terribly cold.
I was outside St Paul's.
About three a.m. a foreign journalist asked me,
'Are you here to honour your great leader?' and I told him.
'No, I usually sleep on the other side,
But tonight it is rather crowded.'
I was glad of morning,
Bringing a lot of young black Ambassadors
In very big cars; then Admirals,
Field-Marshals, Marshals of the Royal Air Force,
In smaller ones, driven perhaps by their wives,
Dusty, up from the country.
The President of Israel
Walked.
At the end I recall how the playing-card Heralds
Emerged from the cathedral

And opened their royal flush across the sooty façade,
Dragons and Pursuivants, red and gold on the grey,
And I thought, 'This is the last time
London will be the centre of the world.'

Unequal to epics,
I should be writing something nobler.
At least I was there...
And afterwards, I remember on television
The soldiers lifting the coffin on to the barge,
And the cranes dipping in honour along the river,
And a workman's voice, not meant to be heard,
Saying,
'Lower, Jim, you can get 'em lower than that.'
Praise indeed, from the wharfside.

59
In Memory of Peter Small, Underwater Explorer, and His Wife Mary

News came your Icarus of the sea was dead.
Out of the dust unkind to other men,
Out of the drift those eager movements rise,
Enthusiast's response, and dancing eyes,
Young Triton's quick dexterity and grace,
Who lived for challenge and took on the sea;
And finding there sufficient adversary
Pursued no other, of class or creed or race,
And spoke fists closed, as if for ever fighting
Against some shadow-sparring sprite or element.

I had imagined his experiment;
Pictured him sidling along shafts of lighting
Across the sea-bed's crowded drawing-room,
A web-toed master of the zebra gloom,
Tugging at weeds and waiting for the peals
From drowned cathedrals; taking whales for strolls,
A swaying shade in blizzards of bright shoals,
Nuzzled by dolphins, corraler of seals;
Or frisking bareback on a bucking shark,
Cowboy and pioneer of submarine rodeo.

What lures the lemming, beams the salmon home?
He might have told us, radared all those dark
Intuitive migrations; gone to town
In Klondikes of the herring; Everests down
Struck oil, or gold, and been our Marco Polo
And colonist and rancher of that cold
Opaque promiscuous weald now free to hold
Secure for one life more, its El Dorado,
Seal up its sperm and clutch its sunk Cathays,
Caves, shelves, mines, forests, fells, till the next challenger.

Sea-widow, and companion of his danger,
Sharer of dreams, child with the mermaid face,
Alone ashore, at every tide alone,
You lent the deceiving oceans, that intone
For those they down their unfelt requiem,
The truthfulness of tears, and have not stayed
To watch life's scarf he waved a muffler frayed
Round old plucked necks, adventure's diadem
Fall to the money-grub, or the timorous,
Saving their pensioned breath, hoard oxygen against age.

Memory's all that's left; and words to rage
For love and daring and life, co-terminous,
Vainly assailing chance as vainly he,

As Icarus the sun, assailed the sea;
Words, to praise all who outleaped instruments
And gave no height, drowning, no deep their name;
Then join her hands with his and close the tomb,
And speaking to the absence, to the silence,
From the far side of tears, remember them
Where sun-dust dances; when the Eroica is played.

Mary Small was born Mary Miles, daughter of G. H. Miles, pilot, millionaire, and self-made founder of Miles Aircraft. Her mother was Blossom Forbes-Robertson, daughter of the actor-manager Sir Johnston Forbes-Robertson and one of the first women to get a degree in aeronautics. The Mileses were very great friends of my wife, who managed the London office of Miles Aircraft before our marriage. Until Mary Miles met Peter Small, a friend of hers wrote to me, she had been thought rather stand-offish, not specially attractive; and unlikely to marry. She came to Peter on someone's recommendation as a secretary, and he transformed her. She was twenty-three and went on his diving adventures with him.

Peter was thirty-six, a grammar school boy from Selby in Yorkshire, where his father had a fish-and-chip shop. He became an underwater explorer and science journalist and for a time a rather unorthodox captain in the Army, in command of a skiing unit. He founded a local branch of the Sub-Aqua Club. Some years after his death the club set up an annual trophy in his honour; the local newspaper wrote of him that he thought of underwater diving as a means to an end as well as an end in itself and 'dreamed of farming a rich harvest of fish and ores beneath the sea' (hence some of the lines in my poem).

My Mary and I went to Mary Miles and Peter's wedding in September 1962, and on 12 October to the exuberant and crowded reception Mary's parents gave for them at Claridge's. They went off together, radiantly happy, to a diving exploration in the Mediterranean, and then, ten weeks later, to Santa Carolina Island, off the coast of California, for work. It was to have been Peter's last dive.

He wanted to test a new gas for use in the diving-bell and also break the underwater diving record. Peter and a mate dived to 1,000 feet. Mary, on board a small ship, watched through closed-circuit television. Something went wrong with the bell-hatch. The two men were brought up unconscious; Peter's mate survived, but Peter died ashore in hospital. Mary returned to London. Her parents did all they could, offered her all they could, but she wished to remain in the flat she had shared with Peter. Relays of friends, disturbed by her silences, stayed nights with her, gave her meals. I began a poem in Peter's memory and sent her from Wales an early version of the verses as they stand now, about him. She replied in a wonderful, reassuringly composed letter on 11 January 1963, that she was trying to go on with some of his pioneer work, so that 'people will remember it was he who started it'. She did not know, she wrote, how I had 'managed to understand him so exactly', and I answered that it was because he had the Commando spirit. Friends told me she was recovering from shock. They gave a party for her in February and on the 21st she sent messages to several, making plans for the future. It seemed safe to leave her to herself for the night. But the next morning she was found dead on the sofa in the sitting-room. She had blocked all the doors and windows, surrounded herself with photographs of Peter and turned on the gas.

I changed the poem into one for both of them. In March we had a telephone call in Wales that it had won the 1973 international Keats Poetry Prize. I recited it at the prize-giving, and it was published in a book with other entries, but (so far as I am aware) nowhere else until here. It gave some kind of solace (I know from letters) to the families of Mary and Peter. Howard Sergeant, editor of Outposts, *was the judge.*

60
Funeral of a Scrap-Man

Old dealer, trumped at last,
All bluffing past.
Now no Arabian tale
Will get you out on bail;
No yarn of a raw deal or a quick sale,
No fantasy now avail.
Game's up, die's cast.

Conmen and conned resort
To this last court,
With all who conned ourselves, about anything –
Thought we could write, or sing,
Seduce, get rich, preach, paint, or play the King –
Living imagining
Some fond false thought.

Those who set grander snares,
Take the front chairs
Quacks of Apocalyptic themes,
Criminal Polyphemes,
Who slaughtered millions for their one-eyed dreams.
Old man, none of your schemes
Did harm like theirs.

Bronze tongue that charmed distrust,
Condemned to rust,
How will you fare, in for so long a spell?
Whom kid, whom undersell,
Homeric scallywag, in the asphodel?
What tall tales tell,
Now that you're dust?

61
A Correspondence

At no time lovers, though they could have been,
They corresponded often, met not much.
Think of harp-music: life the strings between;
One mind; two hands, that play but need not touch.

62
Two Women

Two women who loved one man,
And the man dead,
And the women talking...
Like a sea that shares two shores,
Calm now and warm, coming from great depths,
Waves that make little sound,
And seem hardly to break, telling each shore of the other.

63
Visits from Would-be Biographers

FOR EDITH RUSSELL, IN MEMORY OF
BERTRAND RUSSELL

Great windows. For great views. She dreams…
Someone is throwing pebbles, that fall far short.
In comes one thrower, really at the door.

'I'm here, as promised, for the diary.
I've questioned everyone. Old foes, old friends.
Old flames of course, and just in time for some.
The undertaker's next.
You last, as first. The diary.

The diary. That final year. May I take notes?
A few mistakes. "That radiant day" of yours.
It wasn't Saturday. Forgive me, but I've checked.
Five weeks among the archives. An amazing man…

Just a few points ……………………………………
……………………………………………………
…………Not tiring you, I hope ……………………
……………………………………………………
……………………………………Well, I'll be off.
I hope you'll like the book. I've promises
Of simultaneous publication in the States.
Perhaps a film.
Not tired you, I do hope. You've been marvellous.
It's been an honour for me.'

And the door is closed.
Ears closed, to hear one voice.
Eyes closed, to see one face.

Survivors read at night, or in the dark
They lie at peace, or almost,
One hand across the heart,
One arm stretched out across an empty space.

Bertrand, 3rd Earl Russell (1872–1970), grandson of Liberal Prime Minister Lord John Russell, was the most eminent, some might say the greatest British mathematician and philosopher of the twentieth century; also a brilliant writer and wit who, during his very long life, polemicised against pretty well every Church and important political party in Britain and the United States, and now and then against himself, and ended with the Order of Merit and a Nobel Prize for Literature. Edith Finch, an Anglophile American scholar, twenty-nine years younger and still very attractive, became his fourth wife and the only one with whom he never ceased to be happy. They came to be our neighbours in Wales and very dear to us. I miss them both constantly. After Bertie's death, and then after Mary's, I paid many visits to Edith, and have a sheaf of letters from her. I gave her the poem after Mary's death; the final lines were for us both.

The lacunae in this poem stand, speaking generally, for the kind of ordeals many widows, and presumably widowers, of the famous must expect to undergo.

It came as a shattering blow to me, while preparing this book, to learn of the deaths of both Conrad Russell, Bertie's second son and heir, and his wife Elizabeth. I felt the same affection for them as for Bertie and Edith, and thought of them as having the same 'entirely' loving relationship (see Appendix). I once told Elizabeth that, if Conrad were ever found guilty of a dishonourable act, or a dishonest conclusion in his historical writings, I should seriously begin to think the world was coming to an end, and she agreed. When he turned from history to politics, as spokesman in the House of Lords for the Liberal Democrats, he gave a dignity and authority to Parliament his father would have been proud of; as witness the throng of members who attended the memorial service and heard the splendid speeches for Conrad in St Margaret's, Westminster, Parliament's parish church.

When Professor Alan Monk's biography of Bertrand Russell came out Conrad was disinclined to talk about it, except, anyhow with me, to comment how much he missed from it any inkling of Bertie's sense of fun; as I do also, remembering the so happy succession of evenings Mary and I spent with Edith and Bertie. They were made all the happier by the reconciliation with Conrad, after a separation from childhood onwards of more than twenty years after his mother's divorce. I wish Conrad could have lived to write about his father. He would have been loving, but strict and fair, and certainly out of agreement with many of his policies and opinions. So was I. At the time of the Cuban crisis in 1962, for example, I did not think, as some of his followers did think, that but for his intervention World War Three would have begun. I did think that his correspondence with Khrushchev had given the Soviet leader a means of indicating readiness to compromise. (And what other private individual in any country today has the stature to do that with one, as then, of the two most powerful men in the world?) He gave Mary and me encouragement to hope. Accordingly we took him some roses by way of thanks; and when he advanced saying. 'I don't consider that I have altered the course of history by one iota', I replied that I agreed. I neither expected nor met disapproval or disappointment from him or Edith, then or later; I mention this because the incident has been recorded in several places, and their reaction wrongly interpreted. His life was not, to my mind, 'determined on its course...by colossal vanity' (see Appendix, p. 220). I suggested to him once, when we were more than usually short of funds, that I should compose an essay insulting him, to which he would compose an answer; we would then publish both in a small book and share the proceeds. He replied, 'Oh, but I might agree.' I regret now, noticing some of the charges brought against him, that we did not take ourselves seriously at the time and go ahead.

64
For Moura Budberg

ON HER PROPOSED DEPARTURE FROM ENGLAND

Yes, age deserves
Some quiet, as had youth –
Or so you've told us.
Is that the truth?
Is it a fact
That Talleyrand adored you,
And for your want of tact,
In the Commune of eighteen-seventy,
Marx praised and Eugénie deplored you?

Old ships look home
To harbours they once knew.
Had you such harbours?
Honestly, weren't you
There at Pompeii,
Saved out of the lava
By your great love-to-be?
Did you have words with Madame Bovary?
And weren't you Tolstoy's girl at Balaclava?

Brilliant balloons
Of fantasy and gossip
Inflate to legends.
Till we make up
Twenty, not one,
Swans to whom you were Leda.
How well *did* you know Solomon?
And was he wise? In Berlin, certainly,
The Kaiser took you for the Queen of Sheba?

That you were born
Is also sure, and bred
In deepish purple.
You preferred red.
Grey's not your wear,
London not yours to mate in,
Not now, not any more.
Too many rats. Where to then, citizen-
Baroness, what fresh fields to nest in?

What country to appease
So hungry a delight
In one friend, or many,
Tracing all night
To some old thought
Contemporary ferment;
The Revolution, or the Court;
Talking your casual documentary,
Where every scene seems happening that moment?

Well, join your son.
Give the last party,
And vanish, placing
In the last taxi
Their books men signed,
The letters in the folders,
London's mists left behind,
Your massive shadow fitly lengthening
Not on a grey wall but a golden.

Let it be Italy.
There you'll have snow,
And there'll be moujiks;
Bells, like Moscow,
And just as before
A family to love you,

And riots, and the poor,
And days to dream of the victorious
Sunflower of Russia who once blazed above you.

Baroness Budberg was a grande amoureuse, *born in Ukraine, of an aristocratic family. Her first husband, Count Benckendorff, a Counsellor in the Imperial Russian Corps Diplomatique, was murdered during the Revolution. Maxim Gorky, the Russian writer and friend of Lenin, protected her in Moscow when the Revolution was at a very dangerous height. She accompanied him into exile in Sorrento, arranged for him by Lenin, and presided over his household there for many years. On his return to Russia, she came to England, became the lover of H. G. Wells, and died in 1974. Baron Budberg was an obscure figure, and her marriage to him a fiction to get her to the West. I asked her what became of him, to which she replied, 'I procured him a first-class single ticket to South America.' In the poem 'the sunflower of Russia who once blazed above you' is Gorky.*

65
The Skater

IN MEMORY OF MAURICE HARRISON,
KILLED IN THE ASSAULT ON ST NAZAIRE

Saturday night most people go to the rink.
The lovers with crisscross arms
Check and swing,
Swing and check,
And the band plays the Emperor Waltz;
Till I think of muffs and snow,
And tight little boots, and absorbed

In the midst
With a spiral of short black skirt,
That swerves on a long white thigh,
The partners circle and twirl.

And among them one perfect skater,
Rapt, as if sailed by wireless,
Skims like a skiff, like a swift, with avoidance effortless
Reefing, releasing, leashing, unravelling
Speed,
And spins round the rink.

Often and often I think
Of the pause, the leap into air,
The spark of the steel-blue skate
That spun in the figure of eight,
On and on, till the ice lay bare,
And the sweepers came with their sticks, night falls, and
The end of his day
Lifts,
Lifts and takes,
Lifts, transfigures, and takes him away.

66

A Veteran Returns to Europe

Is this defenceless port the place
That once I came to wreck?
Is nothing manned at our approach,
And no one armed on deck?

No, nothing now's afloat to sink,
Nor on the shore to invade.
Those in the coach are teachers.
These in the ships want trade.

Over old unhappy things
Pacific ledgers mount.
Deals must have duplicates, and lives,
That had none, also count.

And children come with flowers
To place where teachers bid,
Who never heard of Goebbels,
Nor ask what Goering did.

O glittering wings, so suddenly
High in the vacant blue,
Stay, till today dies peacefully,
And normal nights ensue.

Never again the premature!
The anguish, never again!
A rose for those who went in first
And where they fell, remain.

GROUP SIX

How little, in practice and effect, was to become of my first 'aspiration'! It had begun with a mission 'to save the world', progressed through various socio-political experiences (unemployment, the huge changes wrought by the war, Communism in Hungary), and survived in (apart from some of my prose writings) a wish to commemorate my comrades killed at St Nazaire. The four poems that begin this group relate to it. The first of the four is separated from the second and third by about half a century. The fourth bids my first 'aspiration' a regretful goodbye; leading into the rest of the group, which have to do with my second longing, for requited love.

Here is the first. It is about an experiment in practical commemoration of my comrades, launched soon after I had given up journalism and gone to live with Mary in Wales. I put money my father had left me into reviving a mussel fishery off the coast a couple of miles from our home. I hoped with the help of a small group of fishermen to form a cooperative that would reproduce the Commando spirit in peacetime. The poem is a prayer to the Almighty for more working capital, in the venture's early days, before it became a millstone and nearly bankrupted us.

67
Please!

O God, do something worldly for us!
O, load us with a very large sum of money
Now,
And in any reliable currency
Allow
Us to be surprised. Fill up our dustbins
With packages of undevalued
Yen,
Reichsmark, or the more humbly pursued

Pound.
Begin
Each day with the
Sound
Of a not small cheque.
Let
Paul Get-
-ty and Barbara Hutton take a fancy to either or both of
us.
Thrus-
-t several remunerative and gay
Tempta-
-tions in our way,
Such as a
Venice palazzo with a whale-
-scale swimpool, and a
Merc,
Or two Mercs. Arrange for my
Work
To be high-
-ly app-
-lauded everywhere, and re-
-warded beyond its merits. Snap
Thy magnificent fingers, be
Not skimping with largesse,
Tax-free;
For example, gold
Francs,
And from untold
Swiss rolls and credits in countless
Banks,
O God, withhold
Not
O not withhold Thy hand.
But
With such mundane meaningless things, Almighty,

Cover us thick,
Ageing babes-in-the-wood, and
Cover us quick!

The project failed quite soon as a cooperative. I turned it into a limited company, of a benevolence that in most markets would have made it unrecognisable as a business. The prayer had to be repeated in several hours of need and was so regularly answered in the nick of time that the company lasted fifteen years before being honourably put into voluntary liquidation.

The second and third poems could be called political, but relate to no action. I have joined no Party, stood for no Council, taken part in few demonstrations, except, at one time, for Amnesty International. The poems belong to the present day, about fifty years on after the beginning of the fishery, and have to do with the permanent crisis in the Near East, 9/11, and the involvement of Great Britain and the United States in Iraq. The first takes a look, also lighthearted, or fairly, at the so-called special relationship between those two countries. It struck me that the crisis was, and in 2005, with the suicide bombing in London, still is, so appalling that men of very great stature are needed to cope with it. In my youth the two protagonists had been Franklin Roosevelt and Winston Churchill; representation at the top has changed since then, and, it seems to me, not for the better. I should add that I have never been to Springfield, or dreamed of it; it is the title because Abraham Lincoln was born there. Adlai is Adlai Stevenson, once Democrat candidate for President, Vachel is the balladist-poet Vachel Lindsay, Ed Murrow (for me) the *journalist. Also, for any who take the whole poem literally, I do know the geography of the USA better than some lines might suggest.*

68

Dreaming of Springfield

I shan't go to the States. My joyous city,
Springfield Illinois, I cannot today equate
With the dream I had. My singing image
Of lion-cub Lincoln is damaged, of minstrel Vachel
Chortling to Boy Bryan on a May morning,
Immortal phantoms of Edgar Lee Masters,
And dandy Adlai my bantam egghead,
All dead.
I wouldn't be welcome, unless for brandy
With Mrs Buttermire, who said, 'No one at Harvard
Listens the way you listen. Speak.
Speak English', and suddenly shrieked,
'SPEAK…! in that beautiful voice!'
                                                I shan't go
To be quaint, or expect homage to quaintness;
Or to patronise;
Or tell them the wise in Europe are those who've stayed there;
Or regret with a well-bred frown
Some standard they may have let down.
I should have to leave all that alone,
Though I… ah, have I not known
                                                The thrill
Of fulfilling President Roosevelt's lifelong yearning
(That charm, that charm),
Giving him my hand, and as he took it
Knowing he had nothing better to live for,
Now he'd met me! All my letters of thanks,
'Dear Franklin, Eleanor, Ike, and General Marshall,
Ed Murrow', all that elite
Have slid into history.

I shan't go to the States
To hint at some vast purgation awaiting them.
Besides, the Last Judgment
Might blow if I went. I'd rather face it at home.
I'll need to have someone I know.

Sweet coz, cheerio.

Here where I am, in Wales,
The madonna bulbs in my mouth
Will not sprout megaphones.
Ancient, and squirrelish
With my hoards from spring and summer,
I can squat in my winter's root;
Dreaming of school, fourteenth-century school,
Where America had no history;
Dreaming of slow-voiced Springfield,
Where William Penn landed, it's open house,
Where the cottonwood does what it does;
And those limestone crags aren't far,
From which the Indians carved
Walt Whitman's face; and the sumach
Is always in leaf; and the whales
Are junketing off Nantucket;
And across Spoon River, through lilac,
On one side the Golden Gates,
Silhouette of New York on the other,
All lit, all the saviour skyscraper States,
With the lights of the Liberal Tradition,
All wearing their Thanksgiving almsgiving clothes.

But I'm scared of that cauldron country,
Whither so many witches have flown,
And what angel hovers, who knows?

And anyhow, who's asked me?

The next and third poem (69) relates to political events during the build-up to war in Iraq. Prime Minister Blair had been right, after the atrocity of 9/11, to go at once to Washington and offer support to President Bush. Retribution against the initiators and perpetrators, Osama bin Laden and al-Qaeda, was imperative for the American government. But the real, the potentially Armageddon issue, was, is, and for years had been Palestine; Palestine came to be shunted on to a sidetrack (later described as the 'road-map'). Way was thus made for other, hidden agenda of American foreign policy, against the vicious but oil-rich tyranny of Saddam Hussein's Iraq, partly on the false grounds that he had been in close association with al-Qaeda. I had intended to join the huge peace-march against the war in London, but was ill at the time, and Mary's granddaughter, my goddaughter Sarina, put me on her card. The poem, written at the time of the march, is more academic and far less indignant than I would make it now.

69

War in Iraq

Pop-groups in English choirstalls, an outmoded hymn
And other oddities discarded, don't compare
(Though more than a fashionable parochial whim)
With what had been happening to God elsewhere.

Russia got mass upheaval.
Out of parameters still medieval
Myriads famished for up-to-date world-cure
Flocked to a godless star.
It's faded now. Once, they had been so sure.

Now other Messianic nations are,
Who've stayed with God. Their God. Some totally abhor

Ours, with or without guitars. Some just think
However, whomever, Westerners adore,
Amongst us God is not, and cannot be.
Prayer begins their day; with us the market-place.
Moneybugs set our pace.
Most of our early morning readings stink.
Love means pornography.
And faith in God? Hypocrisy.

For some of us, open to creed or race,
But not to even old friends' Grand Design,
In any shape, unless sure the target's right,
If ever justice, poverty, and ignorance had a case,
Which justice, ignorance, and comfort must soon face.
And call the whole world in to solve, not fight.
Priority meant Palestine.

It was not there that warriors did move in,
Nor in the world's name. Sidetracked, they seemed to win…
Except that, to their cries,
'Democrats, rise! It's Liberty!',
Nobody rose. There was no mass 'Whoopee!'
The liberated waited.
What they were waiting for was security.
Doubt entered. Hate infiltrated. Down
Went a dream, and up rose flawed humanity,
One flaw being fear, another Great-Power vanity.
One tyrant gone, but for world-peace no crown.

O Gods of visions, who send such chances missed,
Don't let it go on like that! To that appalling list
Don't add Jerusalem, Earth's triple shrine!
Don't chalk up Palestine!
Empower difference and protest to persist
Peacefully. In our littleness
Help Truth and Love, life's reasons to exist.

I pause on the concluding words. Of Love, in different meanings, there are poems among all that follow. For Truth, as a consequence of my experience as a journalist, and as a diligent observer during the Cold War afterwards, I had acquired a passion. I was sick of lies, one in my own life especially, to which I shall come. For the moment I think of political lies, my own again, in the disgraceful ease with which I allowed myself to be taken in by Hitler, for however short a time, with however infinitesimal effect, from which at least I learnt how quickly good intentions pave the road to Hell. I also learned to admit this, and did so in print and on television, and in many conversations, as a warning to others as well as myself. In Hungary, in order to remain there, I tried to report the ruthlessness of the Communists, during their takeover, as facts without comment; and at the same time remind readers at home of injustices by pre-war Hungarian governments without which Communism could not have taken root. As a result, years later, of this attempt at fairness I learnt of secret lies against myself, from both sides, as follow.

When I arrived in Budapest in 1947, Rákosi, the Communist dictator and lickspittle of Stalin, had ordered his then secretary Ferenc Donath, in my presence, to arrange for me to see everything I wished to see. I saw and reported. After I had left, Rákosi was in trouble and needed scapegoats to please Stalin. He picked, among many others, on Donath, a most honourable man. In a closed 'trial', under duress, Donath 'confessed' that he had acted on my orders and given me information as head of British Intelligence and sabotage in Hungary (the information of course contained nothing Rákosi had not ordered Donath to arrange and, almost certainly, read himself years before). Donath was given a long prison sentence for doing what he had been told to do. A short while later Rákosi himself fell from power, and high time. Donath was released. He was recalled to court, where he stated that everything he had 'confessed' about myself had been false. He was 'rehabilitated'. I have never been an Intelligence officer for anyone. Correspondents working under dictatorships had to get used to this kind of thing. What I was not used to was a letter shown me among the newspaper's archives, sent confidentially about the same time to the editor by a very eminent Englishman, to tell him he had proof positive that I was a paid-up member of the Communist Party. That too was a lie. The Times, *as far as I know, had ignored it. In the history of* The Times *my work during that most difficult period was described as 'an exercise in honesty'. This was the truth, and I was grateful for it, as for nearly all my time with them.*

At home, as everyone knows, the pre-war belief in British justice was shown up, about Ireland and other matters, as an illusion. In a succession of notorious trials innocent men were sentenced to many years in prison. Half-truths, evasions, prevarications abounded, while private wishful thinking so congealed in the minds of powerful men that, once in the open, it became hardly distinguishable from lies. In foreign affairs, at the time of the Iraq war I was reminded of Prime Minister Eden and the secretly planned assault on Suez, kept from Cabinet, Parliament, and people; which, we were told after the Americans aborted it, must never happen again. I made my only speech at a big public meeting against it. From my youth I remembered Appeasement. I could never forget, way back before the war, my interview with Geoffrey Dawson, at that time editor, a man I liked, who had given me my first big assignment with the royal tour in Canada and the States; how, after my return, he had suggested I might go to Washington to be trained as correspondent there; my demur, in July 1939, two months before Hitler invaded Poland and war was declared, that I was in the Territorial Army and likely to be called up; and his blithe, incredible reassurance in reply, 'The danger of war is immeasurably removed.' Appeasement may have made sense in earlier years; but at the time the remark, from one of the best-informed and most influential newspapermen in the world, seemed to belong to wishful thinking near the highest level, with repetitive echoes two generations later from Mr Blair about Iraq.

This poem takes metaphorical leave of the failures of my first aspiration. The last verse soon leads on to failures in regard to Mary.

70
Memoirs of My Dream Life

Time I told one and all
What's happened to me.
At seventy won the Grand National.
At eighty agreed,
When Nureyev went weak in the knee,
To star in Les Sylphides.

Learnt physics at ninety-one.
Soon got the answer,
And a Nobel Prize (I go on
Where Einstein stops).
At ninety-five cured cancer,
At a hundred was top of the pops.

President, PM, for a spell,
I had to decline
Reconciling Araby, Israel,
Russia and China,
Had other ideas at the time.
Went to work as a miner.

Built homes for the homeless,
Reformed the post,
Rendered bureaucracy harmless,
Cleaned up New York,
Saved what was left of our coast,
Found everyone work.

All in all I can say,
Achievement has matched
All my boyhood's hopes, all my day-
Dreams, feathers in cap,
Chickens counted before they were hatched
Have fallen into my lap.

Of my private life I won't speak,
Though it's not denied
I preserved a superb physique
To a hundred and ten.
And, darling, you stayed by my side,
Murmuring now and then,

'Don't you imagine, dear love,
Rather more than you've done?'
On the whistle-stop mirage of life
Supporting a man with a ton
Of failures and private faults.

The next poem, early and lighthearted, ends with a promise to Mary I failed to keep. It was prompted by a contemporary anthology.

71
Twentieth-Century Poetry

'Poets represented
In this collection:
Auden Betjeman Empson
Graves MacNeice Stevie Smith
Watkins Davie and Gunn
Hughes (O Hughes) Jennings and Larkin

Logue Moraes Tomlinson
Thwaite Barker and Blackburn
Causley Gascoigne and Graham
Stubbs Kavanagh Dylan Thomas
Etcetera.' Who is Etcetera?
A pseudonym? A woman.
Señora Etcetera.
Lives in Madrid. Knew Hemingway.
Smokes cigars.
Transvestite.
No? Then Scandinavian?
Hedda Ingeborg
Oxenstierna Etcetera.
Used to haunt waterfront bars.
Drowned herself in a fjord.
No? Then a movement, a clique,
Dedicated to the purity
Of direct obscurity
As against the oblique.
Wrong again? Well, who?

Darling, it's you!
'Represented in this collection!'
And you never let on.
'Not for sale in the USA.'
Why not?
You who have seen such a lot.
You who have got
So much to say –
Why not?

The next poem, 'Nehemiah', sited in Palestine and about a hero of Jewish history in the Old Testament, is a keystone in the book and means much to me. Mary wrote piercingly in letters about some of my poems; but 'Nehemiah' and the last in this group, 'Till Doomsday', are the only two on which I remember, remember vividly, her verbal comment. After I had read it to her, 'But this is something quite different!' she exclaimed. It had moved her. I did not ask her why, and she did not tell me. I wrote it in one of the two cottages in North Wales, Melin Parc (The Mill) and Tan-y-Clogwyn (Under the Rock), which she and her great friend Peter Lindsay had restored before the war. I used to think that the poem had moved her because two men who had been in love with her, and had connections with Palestine, had spent brief spells of peace in the cottages. Both were writers and both had written classics. In 1938 she had lent the Mill cottage to George Antonius, gifted and dedicated champion of the Palestinian cause; he finished his The Arab Awakening *there. In the summer of 1942 she spent a blissful week at Tan-y-Clogwyn with Richard Hillary, the young fighter-pilot, whose account of the Battle of Britain,* The Last Enemy, *had just come out. Brought down in 1940, blinded and terribly burnt, he had been treated by Sir Archibald MacIndoe in his hospital at East Grinstead; had persuaded, almost forced the authorities to allow him to return to flying, and was killed on training with night-fighters in January 1943. He had decided that he must return after reading* The Mint, *the account T. E. Lawrence 'of Arabia' published privately about his own enlistment in the RAF. In an unwitnessed will Hillary bequeathed to Mary the portrait of him by Eric Kennington, close friend and painter of Lawrence and several of the Arab leaders; she gave it to his parents and it is now in the National Portrait Gallery. She had told me about Antonius and Hillary, and I had read and admired their books. It would have been impossible for her not to have been reminded of them by my poem. But it has more to do with her own relationship with me, who had no connection with Palestine at all. Here it is with an interpretation at the end.*

72
Nehemiah

[He was a Jewish exile in Babylon, who became cup-bearer to King Artaxerxes about the middle of the fifth century BC. Given leave to go back to Jerusalem to rebuild the city walls, he rebuilt them in fifty-two days, despite attacks on his men and intrigues by neighbouring tribes, and remained governor for twelve years. But for him, the Jewish religion and nation might not have survived.]

By Nehemiah the Governor,
Given from Zion.

Yes, tell our friends in Babylon,
We have done well with the walls.
Peril, hard toil,
Guerrillas, the people squabbling,
But we have done well. And when I recall
The corner-stone, whose arch will be Heaven, and recall
The grit, and think of the pearl,
It was worth the fierce dry wind.
We have rebuilt Jerusalem.

By the walls of Jerusalem
I sat down.
I tried not to weep.

Suppose it had been Babylon destroyed,
And Jerusalem our exile.
Suppose us returned from Jerusalem
To rebuild Babylon's walls.

How can I think such a thing!
How can I hold it back!

Longing to merge, with all life, easily;
Not to be always apart,
Not to be one God's only.

While it was still safe to sleep outside,
Before the guerrillas started,
Sleepless in my tent,
The young dozing beside the camp-fires,
I would become aware of the cedar-scent,
And music. Did I dream music?
Were the musicians dreaming?
Fingers sleepwalking the strings
With yearnings not our yearnings;
Fire on a young man's face,
Fire on a girl's breast,
Like an orange in his lap...

An Arab rode down from Lebanon,
Mountains strange to us, where they know what it means
To be frozen,
Singing so hauntingly.
Daylong, nightlong, I falter
Under this terrible strain of being chosen.

Chosen for what?
Paramours of the Nameless One.
Does He need us, or we Him?
What is Evil?
Answer, explain.

O, could I mingle the soft
Cinnamon-scented wind with the fierce wind
Blowing off Sinai, guide them
Like water, have conduits as for water,
To compel them into one course!

The holocaust steams up.
Twelve years during all my governorship
I have not taken my salary,
Nor claimed my expenses,
Nor bought up poor men's land;
Have stood with the builders
Against the arrows of the wrong-doers;
Seen to it the law was read and expounded
To the whole people, who wept
In the great square in front of the Temple,
But soon forgot they had wept.

People for ever reverting, falling away...
Babylon.
Arms that reach and entice.
World without mission,
World of seaweeds of gold,
Rivers of power, desire,
And we so far from the sea,
Saturated in prophecies,
Jeremiah Isaiah,
Whales flailing in the ditch of Jordan!
I, who remember Euphrates...
The mighty estuaries,
Slowly entering sea, shuddering, trembling,
Caressed by hands of the scented wind,
Withdrawing leaves on the supine sands
Pools that are memories of touch.
Babylon...
Babylon!
Nights that I bore the cup to the spade-beard King
In the great palace at Shushan
Among tolerant Gods, who permitted other Gods.
With markets and elephants and the columned banquet,
Jewels, astronomers,
The three hundred and sixty-five positions of Eros,

The two winds of Love, the dry one catching me up
Whirled me on my face at the Great King's feet,
Weeping, imploring,
'Send me!
Send me to Zion!'

And God sent him to send me,
With timber from the King's park for the gates of Zion
And an escort of cavalry.

Remember me, O God, for good.

Have I not dedicated the walls,
Walking behind the choir along the top of the walls
Over the rebuilt gates,
With all the priests blowing trumpets,
The cantors and thousands of the people
Rejoicing, singing so loud
The Moabites heard them?
Have I not scoured from the Temple
The branch office of a heathen bank,
Restored an undefiled priesthood,
Enforced the Sabbath?
When a boy and girl went walking
I rebuked them: 'Why are you not in the Temple?'
And he tapped his heart and replied,
'The Temple is here.'

But it cannot be.
Priesthood without which nothing can survive;
Temple of stone, without which all is in vain;
Walls enclosing the heart,
Essential ritual, accretions,
Piled bone upon bone, of the Law,
Have kept our God one rock
In a flux of nations, till the rock in its own time

Fashion us also into a nation again.
O ossifications, rules,
Priests all with the same face, people
All praying the same prayer,
Giving receiving the same penalties,
I say you are necessary!
I say that without you
We shall go under, dissolve.
Be even more alike! Strike
Out of our liturgy the lovely idyll of Ruth,
Root out the alien marriage,
Pure ones, elect,
Seed of Abraham, multitudinous as the stars.

Rhetoric.
Our toil vain.
All, one day, will be scattered again.
The walls will be levelled. Nothing
So four-square can survive.
Only the winds survive.

Cool mountains of Lebanon,
Waters of Lebanon, cool.
By Jerusalem's dark cypresses,
By the meagre pool,
I sat down,
I wept,
When I remembered you.

I wrote this poem many years after certain heart-searing but brief periods in Mary's and my life together. It was, and is, important to me much less for the lines concerned with Nehemiah's achievement, which are a poetic elaboration of the account of him in the Old Testament, than for the passages I imagined. I re-invented him as a man with a mission from God, which he was, but deeply troubled, as he never was, by moods in which he wishes he was without it; questions it; fantasises about giving it up and returning to the privileged life he had enjoyed in Babylon; and in the concluding lines is beginning to believe that, even if he continues and fulfils it, sooner or later it will be forgotten, evaporate...'only the winds survive'. It is a poem about the closing-in of despair.

I go back for my interpretation to an idyllic week Mary and I had spent in 1946, while we were still lovers. Throwing conventions, responsibilities, to the winds, she had come out to join me in Austria. Approaching Vienna I had taken her to the top of the Kahlenberg, the wooded hill that towers above the city, and shown her the Danube, stretching into the East like a destiny, and she had put in her diary, 'I have a feeling of having lived all this before. I take his hand and it is warm and strong. A great sense of power seems to flow between us – that together it would always be like this – that together we could move mountains and achieve great things.' Afterwards I had sent two telegrams imploring her to marry me, and a letter reminding her how wonderful it had all been, and marriage and the future would be, adding almost casually that there had still been moments when I had felt I was incapable of loving anyone. She had taken this up and a correspondence followed, in which both of us were thinking of things that might destroy a marriage. I feared my sexuality. She did not answer this directly. What she wanted was to give the decision 'a little more time'. Out of her thoughts at night she wrote, 'From your point of view the most important thing is to have a child...I would not marry you without the certainty of a child.' She had consulted her doctor Tibor Csato, a confidant of many years, and he had told her there was nothing against her having a child. 'If I had been sure beyond all doubt when we were together in Austria,' she wrote, 'I would have risked having one and then we would have married with a life to enrich our love...At other times I wake and feel that my life is irrevocably linked with yours...and then (equally strongly) that the difference in our ages, <u>that one thing</u>, could affect the fundamental perfection and destroy us.' It was something I scarcely considered. In Poem 18 I had described her as a miracle, and this continued. I too *believed my life irrevocably linked with hers. I understood that I would have to wait, and so we waited. Finally I wrote to her that I wanted a child by her as an act of faith in the future. She answered that this 'brought me together with you as never before. It meets something fundamental in me and springs into a life-force between us.' We married on 27 March 1947, anniversary of the raid on St Nazaire. Not long afterwards she had to go into hospital. When I went in to see her, Tibor met me and told me she was out of danger. I never knew what had happened. What it meant was that she could not have a child, sad for me, heart-breaking for her. And then this poem.*

73
Children

Not for the statesman's laurels,
Not the heroic palm,
The hopes that once sustained us,
When love was slow to warm.
And nearer now, and clearer,
Since hopes too came to harm,

We see, through old misfortunes,
Hurt young is hurt for good.
My vines won't grow on your hillside.
My grapes are stained with your blood...
These songs at last, my sea-spray,
Flowering on your flood.

So late our light, so different
From lives that find at morn
Contenting plough and pasture
And home at dark return,
With never a crop not lifted,
And never a lamb not born.

Many people, men and women, have surrendered a family life in favour of some other creative purpose: art, science, politics, many kinds. But what if, in a partnership, one partner, willingly or unwillingly, forgoes children (Mary, in our case, unwillingly) for the sake of a mission or vocation credited to the other (myself as writer), and the other, for one of many possible reasons, proves unequal to it and that goes too?

It has been an irony that, for more than half a long life, I, with my 'passion for truth', should have consented or was compelled by British law and convention and, after the law was changed, convention, to live a lie; except with Mary and a few friends (and unfriends to whom I disclosed my sexual nature). It had become clear to me quite soon that my moving of Poem 13, 'Most Happy Creature', from its true time and place of origin in Colditz to that moment in England when I first made love to Mary and imagined that all my gay desires would vanish, had been wishful thinking of a high order. In spy-thronged Budapest, where The Times *had sent us, yielding could have been disastrous; besides, other people's troubles engrossed our own anxieties and brought us closer. London was different. London offered opportunity. Desire attacked quite soon, in gathering force, the kind of force described in the next poem. One night, when Mary was away, I gave in and was trapped by two blackmailers. About midnight, after they had made their demands and left me, taking papers of mine with them, I rang Tibor. He was at home and I went at once to see him. In the morning he put me in touch with a lawyer; as a result I told the police what had happened. Tibor told Mary I was having a slight breakdown due to overwork, and was best left on my own, and she went for a week or two to her sister's. The case was heard first at a magistrates' court, myself appearing as Mr X for the prosecution, and then, on appeal, at the Old Bailey, in all about nine months of intense strain. The blackmailers were sent to prison. The psychiatrist to whom Tibor referred me begged me, from experience, not to tell Mary, and for a while, though much against my will, I obeyed. But one night, lying in bed at home, I told her. It took about an hour. She was silent several minutes and then said 'Darling, how awful to have to go through all of that alone.'*

Had she lived, a poem, the one that follows, could have shown her how deep was my sexual dissociation. But she did not need to know. The pattern I was asking of her was unfamiliar, but her mind was as open as her heart. Friends were once discussing same-sex marriages; in her view there was no reason why friendships should not be blessed. I longed to love her wholly, and she believed this; so far as, however painfully, for a while to accept a friend I found – honest, working-class, bisexual, but predominantly for women, whom from time to time I saw; it could only have been for one purpose. It was never an 'arrangement'. She met and liked him, and he was gallant with her. A sign told her when our meetings ceased. I always went to Mass with her, but never took Communion. Until one morning I did. Elsewhere I have told how, laughing, her eyes shining, she exclaimed, 'Why didn't you tell *me?'*

I give the poem, nonetheless. Originally it was called 'After Leaving', from the true occasion, many years after her death, which prompted it. I renamed it, because rejection had been so large a part of my sexual experience; just as later, after her divorce, having to reject had been of hers.

74
Rejection

I

Twilight. In the dark wood young fauns,
Lithe shadows of faint bronze,
Children of sun, living in darkness,
Lean towards him and whisper,
'The one you seek is there,
Alone in the house. Go in.' He sees the satyrs,

Old and wise, but fearful of them,
Mouthing, 'Don't go'. But goes.
And is rejected.
The fauns are dancing now. 'Join us!' they cry.
'We have all that there is for happiness.'
But he does not go.
And it is as it always is... the Consolers waiting.

2

Will the hills not help? Lift up your eyes...
I will not.
The hills can't help.

Or the sea?
You'll be passing the Bay. It's stormy.
You can strip and swim...
I have done that.

But if something sensational happened?
A unicorn coming sidling up
With a free ticket stuck to its horn
To Enchanted Ground...?
Forget it.

Have you never considered hunchbacks
Or those about to be tortured? There are things
Far worse...
Than this
Nothing is worse.

You can go for fame.
Michelangelo, Proust, all the rest
Could never have been what some of them became
Without a distress like yours. You can drink it away,
Or inject...

I
Have woken up on the floor,
A hole in my forehead, ink
And blood on my shirt, on the
Floor. I have walked by a
Certain lake, stones in my
Pockets, a hundred times,
With a note a
Hundred times torn up…

You have surely heard
Of Love-For-Its-Own-Sake?

Yes.
It is useless.
There will always be someone
To possess whom one cannot desire,
Or desire whom one cannot possess.

Then how will you go on living?

Let the grief rage. Let me ride
The black horse and be thrown,
Nuzzled, trampled, to hear it canter away
Out of boredom. To throw someone else,
And the hills and the sea,
Ambition, unicorns, suicide,
Exhaust someone else's pride.
This assault has failed, and I
Can stand up and say,
'It has passed. It has passed. It has
passed.'
Though it has not passed….

Not yet?

And never will.

From later years I could also have shown Mary another poem. It is about Despair, a sour plant native to Rejection, a sour soil. The last line is one of the keys to interpreting 'Nehemiah'.

75
The Visit

Despair came to my door the other day.
This was the guest I had said jokingly
Had never come, and I'd write better with.
Send me a visit from Despair, I'd said.

Despair moved in on me the other day,
Grey-faced, grey-blooded; swept
Off my lush stage my smirking plot of life,
And wheeled across bare boards a sneering opposite;

Showed me my once love dead, and dead for ever,
Played me that trite and savage vaudeville...
Desire each morning greener in heart and mind,
And body mocking them; charade

After mocking charade, mask after mask,
That I had thought my face, but all were masks
Hanging on pegs of years like shrivelled heads;
And on the last hung Faith.

Faith was a mask...
O God, what freezing grey that visit brought!
We are the facts you would not face, it said.
Angel, my archangel, spear-shining Michael,

Make them not so, love I still crave to live.
Marshal me into verse, should panic come

Again, to me, stalked by Despair that day.
And all you poor, and sick,

Forgive the slick mood that invited him,
Prisoners, exiles, all Despair's familiars,
Forgive, who have no love, no friends, no comfort,
Nor blessed anodyne of relief in words.

The Nehemiah I had invented despaired. I was alone at Tan-y-Clogwyn, and near despair, because of my sexuality and because 'the blessed anodyne of words' was failing me. It was all but impossible to write. The blackmail case had been settled in late autumn, the time when the season for mussel fishing begins. Mary understood the idealistic motive that had prompted the idea of a fishery and approved the healthy life, but not other managerial duties someone else not yet found would have done better. In March 1957 I had to prepare a balance sheet, and she went to London for a spell. She began a long letter late one night, telling me how, one evening at the cottage, she had watched me writing with unusual intensity and... 'Thinking it must be poetry, I held my breath so as not to break the spell. Alas, my imagination was tiptoeing on the ruddy accounts! Perhaps this all sounds more frenzied than I really feel, and it's getting on for 3.30 a.m. and you know things look gigantic at that time...but it seems idiotic for you to spend hours totting up those figures. It's so much worse than me doing all that washing-up and I know how frustrating that is to the spirit.' She used, of herself, glancingly, a phrase, 'a waste of a good life', which shattered me. Awaiting Mrs Lloyd Williams (Poem 31, aka Mrs Williams Pugh) with milk, I sent off a cri de coeur to London. The date is 23 March 1957.

The fire out, the water stopped, the washing up of generations surging in the kitchen sink, papers and old handkerchiefs sharing the floor with limp gloves of a dying magnolia, a mouse dashing the last crust from underneath two weeks of unread newspapers, my false plate of teeth staring at me from the dresser like a sculpture waiting for a name – and outside no doubt the jungle creeping to the door – all the beauty of order which you leave behind dispelled from the house in order, if ever possible, to be concentrated on what I am writing or not writing – this is the setting in which at present is placed he whom the Vatican and (?) Common Law acknowledge as your husband...

There follow a page or two about the privileges of creative artists, authors especially, to be left alone, citing in support Tolstoy, 'who went away for two years', and then:

Terrible words din in my ears, which you said of yourself, 'It's such waste of a good life'. This I can't forget. There's no doubt I've been near another of those ghastly breakdowns...I have to fight this insistent enemy within myself [my sexuality, not the accounts] before I can even reach the point of embarkation for a work of art...and this, as you know full well, is a sullen hateful black battle, in which the chief wounds are yours... I learn enough in solitude to know what a wilderness the world would be without you. Yet often, when we are together, I seem to lay it waste for you. The reason, we both know, is the witch who came to my christening. It enrages more than saddens me that I should not be equal to you, that because of me a life as rare and glorious as yours should not flower illimitably, you who should have been the love of all the poets and heads of States.

I aspired to a novel nothing less, or not much less than War and Peace, *of which she would be the heroine. 'Perhaps', I ended this familiar literary lament, 'I shall never hear the sound of my own voice.'*

She answered:

You shouldn't let certain words, torn out of unsuspecting depths, din in your ears without remembering the beautiful

> ones that break from the overflowing heart. I know it's difficult to forget the sad and bitter things said in moments of despair or great inner frustration, but to understand the moments of conflict from which they spring should make it easier. Your destructive side comes from the times when you are withdrawn from me and which I understand as far as it is possible to understand something not in one's own realm of experience. I know that at such times you will be destructive and I may react in a destructive manner, but well below we have the great strength of real love and the knowledge that we stand together...I have no fear that you will one day find the way to the sound of your own voice, not through writing of your conflict, but out of your conflict. It is as if all your 'works' so far have been exercises like a pianist practising his technique – and when that is done he is free at last to throw his hat over the moon and create his own world which is his alone.

Not 'of', but 'out of". In all our scores of pages of correspondence, not once does she mention the word 'homosexual' (or 'gay', which may not yet have come in). We were talking once about a gay friend, a writer, a good writer, who seemed to be unable, or else not to wish, to write about anything else. I said, 'I shall have to write about homosexuality one day', and she answered, 'Yes, I know you will. But not too much.' In 'Nehemiah' I had shown a sign of being able to go beyond myself. And beyond my torments about her. Or her beauty, or her 'oasis eyes', or other love-poems I have omitted from this book; she had had enough of all that. In the same letter she wrote of 'so many young writers who start off with some brilliant piece which will have no value for posterity apart from a superficial picture of their particular period in time'. She had chosen to attribute to me an ambition 'not to write exclusively out of your tiny self,' and went on:

> Not to make it personal is to study and understand all the conflicts, pettiness and greatness of human beings in relation to the world in which you choose to place them. Those times

of conflict when you go right down into the blackest depths must have given you a greater understanding of other people's sufferings and terrible moments of despair. It is no good wishing I could help you more at such times. I understand enough to know I can't except by trying not to be upset myself and thereby only making things worse.

Some of my poems began to be published during the late Sixties. Dennis Enright and Dannie Abse encouraged me. In 1973 I was awarded the Keats Prize and the Poetry Book Society made a slim volume their choice. 'Nehemiah' was not in it. I had only read her a draft. But the volume did contain that only other poem on which I 'vividly remember' her comment. Summarising the past, I went back to our relationship. Wishing to thank her for her guidance and patience, in the first part I had put, without being precise about them, an indication of my failings. In the last stanza I gave an undertaking for the future.

76
Till Doomsday

When in my cleverness
I smothered her,
She rose up from the bed,
And put my clothes away.
When in my bitterness
I stabbed her,
She washed away the blood,
And made our bedroom gay.
When in my sullenness
I drowned her,
She walked home by the sands,
And did things needed doing.

Only her eyes showed bruising.
The sea was in her hands,
And loneliness the wound.
She kept a diary that will not be found.
To the world the perfect pair. I've never written
The story of those murders. There has been
No trial, all being frustrate; even
My own upon myself she thwarted. She
Encouraged me to express
My self's excesses less self-centredly...

Hiker or antiquary,
Dragging the ivy from our century,
Know our worn monument
Tells of the world one Irish heart the less,
The gayest Ireland ever sent
To dance on English ground;
And with her me,
By her got ready for eternity.
And any thrush that's heard
In storm or snow, or other quiet bird,
Sings as executor of my will,
And shall until
My debt is quit
For love she gave,
For love she gave,
And gives
Till Doomsday sound.

Mary's comment, relating to the first part, was 'I think you've been too harsh on yourself'. She said no more, perhaps read no more. She was too tired. In fact, though I did not know it at the time, she had begun to die. She died in the following year, 1974. My next slim volume came out five years later. 'Nehemiah' was in it. Many of the other poems, I think, were new, and are away from, or 'out of', rather than 'of' my own conflicts; as are others in this book, written long after her death. To me they show the kind of advance that had made her think 'Nehemiah' 'different', and moved her. It is also possible that the poem delighted her because the hero went on with his mission, and so did we, for thirty-one years, I in life, and she in a second life of memory.

GROUP SEVEN

Instead of, as in the earlier groups, separating the notes in this group one from another, I have incorporated several poems' titles in the long paragraphed note which follows, preceding the poems themselves.

Mary's granddaughter Sarina said to me once, 'Don't make her a saint.' Heaven forbid. Nor a guru, or whatever is the female equivalent. What I learned from her came about most of the time so lightly, casually, in things she happened to say, in her letters, not least in her silences. Listening, to begin with. It seemed that, often alone and in a strange country (Brazil), she had been listening ever since childhood. And afterwards, when some of her women friends' husbands, aware that her marriage was falling to pieces, made up to her and told her how misunderstood they were too. And after that, after she had got her legal divorce (though not in the eyes of the Roman Catholic Church, and in spite of a husband who, in vain, had her followed), men genially took it for granted she must be lonely and need someone. She listened, and disappointed them. She seldom talked about it, but on one rather rare occasion she did tell me of having, at some reception, been introduced to a man renowned for his brilliance, billed even to be Prime Minister, who offered to take her home; and almost before the taxi-driver had got into gear, pounced.

She hated the theory about women possessing some special sixth sense, some 'feeling', some 'intuition', which tells them what people are really thinking. She had studied and stored up what she had learned from listening, and was ready to pass it on, or some of it, if asked. And I, at first so busy telling her of my own way, born in me, of being misunderstood, unfortunately forgot to ask more. Yet always I felt somehow aware of being aware that I was in the presence of wisdom. I came to her as a pupil in dire need, son to a generous, honest, charming, and much-loved but, perhaps unconsciously, chauvinist father, whom my mother loved, but knew she was expected 'to know her place' Only once, after we married, did my mother complain to us of being treated as 'a bloody fool'; and of suggestions made by her and rejected, only to see them adopted and treated as coming from someone else. I should have listened to her, encouraged her; and also my sisters.

For years after we married I still talked too much; but among guests was so often conscious, as if at an unpaid, incidental university, of Mary, one finger pressed to her cheek, and wearing a slight smile, listening. Ages of women took their places in my thoughts, who had either accepted or manipulated their condition. It was a young woman, studying theology, who first brought to my notice that Jesus, after his Resurrection, appeared first to women; and that the apostles treated what the women told them as 'idle tales'. Terribly late, successive waves of feminism reached me, and recent generations of women getting their own back, and men becoming afraid. Late middle age found me ready for the backlash, with phases that had my sympathy. I went to a meeting of Fathers 4 Justice planning a demonstration, like Carbonari in the nineteenth century. At parties I copied Mary's silences, but after her death started to talk too much again. I was invited once to dinner to meet Isaiah Berlin and Roy Jenkins. Driving there, I promised myself to keep quiet in such company; but, driving home alone, recalled having seldom drawn breath. On the whole, however, I had learnt to listen, and my hearing-aids became attuned to both sexes. In these pages Poem 77, 'In the Beginning', is the only fruit.

'Don't make her a saint.' Nor the house, Beudy Gwyn, a shrine. All the same, by now I can see some point in Sarina's hint, uttered some fifteen years ago, sixteen after Mary's death. I have called certain places and houses and beaches, and one waterfall, 'Enchanted Ground', and people have latched on to it. Also by now, during those thirty-one years, I have published one slim volume of poems (1978) with several still about Mary; two books, both documentary, with her as heroine; one, in 1988, with Richard Hillary as her lover, the other, in 2003, my autobiography, with me as her husband; and now these poems, with their 'accompaniment' of notes. I have not been commissioned, nor did I vaguely 'choose' to write any of them. It has just turned out like that.

For example: Goronwy Rees arrived soon after Mary's death;

scholar, writer, Fellow of All Souls, now stricken widower. His own wife, Margie, had just died – of cancer. His daughter Lucy thought I was surviving the better of us two and he should come to Beudy Gwyn. He came, stayed, read Mary's unforgettable farewell to Hillary, and wrote to me that it had been

> *a comfort and a source of hope, so that I feel Margie is not wholly lost and I do not have to live entirely without her. And on Tuesday night I dreamed about her. And she was exactly as she had been before all her pain and suffering, and I felt that the dream was a kind of blessing on Beudy Gwyn and on yourself.*

If a blessing, then on Mary, who created the house, and myself, who have written about and shared it. We were together – in her phrase we had that 'affinity that is not usual' – but we were also separate. That conception was vital to her. Two people, married, in love, real human love, together, and finding their separate, their own ways, to truth, whatever the truth might turn out to be for each of them. In essence, it turned out to be the same.

I wrote 'Eurydice' (Poem 78) for her as a kind of set-piece, a formal 'in memory of', hoarded and altered over many years. The Greek myth tells how the gods give the poet-musician Orpheus leave to bring back his dead wife Eurydice from Hades, provided he never looks round to make sure she is following. My poem imagines them both, as they near the exit, changing places, she going out first, serenely, and myself, as Orpheus, in the last two lines

> *Groping his own way to the way that she,*
> *Who was his light, went into light itself.*

I took the phrase about 'light' from Mary's farewell to Hillary, which is in full elsewhere. In their case he had gone first, and she had been left alone. In our case she went first. For her the way and the light meant Christianity. Also for me, but along a different path. Mary was Irish, Irish Catholic, brought up during her early childhood in Rio de Janeiro. I was English, with two Scots grandmothers, one of them Nonconformist, myself baptised in the Anglican

Communion, and confirmed in Winchester College Chapel, Protestant since the Reformation, hands laid on my well-washed head by the Anglican Bishop of Winchester. At school, as I grew older and reached the top form and studied the ancient classics, not least the great satirist Aristophanes, I imbibed sips and gulps of scepticism from one or two stunning teachers. And thus, I put in my autobiography, my five years there had 'presented me, as child of God and heir to Greece and Rome, with two prescriptions for heart and mind, a double talisman for a life of creative interaction by which, if I wished, I need never cease to grow. Beside this, and taking acquisition of facts for granted, I see all other purposes and results attributed to public schools as secondary.' On top of this twin inheritance, a slow, a very slow discovery of my sexual nature began to make manifest that I had been born an outlaw; literally, until in 1967 the law was modified; anyhow, on a number of other matters that had nothing to do with sex, someone not disposed automatically to obey received rules, opinions, conventions.

In 1941 I had made my first open break, in what many people might think a highly conservative direction. During training with my Commando in the West Country a kindly old German priest had received me, at Buckfast Abbey, into the Roman Catholic Church. There had been no time for thorough instruction; any day, any night, I might be off on a raid and not return. As with many in like case, my sexuality had begun seriously to trouble me. I had no one I could confide in without upsetting them. Secondly, though Hitler had the greatest guilt for the war, all nations involved had their share, and I sought an authority that appeared to be both inter-and supranational. Thirdly, it (I never got used to calling the RC Church 'She') had been in touch with God longer than anyone else, and seemed to have been giving its huge following clear and authoritative answers.

Alone after Mary's death I had continued to go to Mass for at least five years, when two coups de foudre *struck me, by then well into my sixties, which I had never expected or hoped or prayed for. I fell in love twice, with two homosexual men half my age, with an interval of about three years between. Both men reciprocated.*

(Poems 79, 80, 81, 82, 'A Young Knight's Tomb', 'Peace', Absence' and 'Love Continuing', relate to them.) I asked a priest what I should do. He asked me what were my feelings, to which I replied, in my loneliness, immense gratitude. Therefore, he told me, I should give thanks to God, which I have not ceased to do for those and numberless other blessings. But a priest is not the Pope. The Roman Catholic Catechism of 1994, section 2357, states – or reasserts – of homosexual acts that 'under no circumstances can they be approved', and section 2359, 'Homosexual persons are called to chastity'. I could find nothing in the words of Jesus to justify the latter, and felt no such vocation. It seemed that I could no longer consider myself as part of the Roman Catholic community. I did however give and was given love as long as each relationship lasted. Both friends became exceptionally fond of Beudy Gwyn and all it expressed of Mary. I was thus left with my wish to go on considering myself a Christian within a P/protestant (with both a capital and lower-case initial letter) community where I felt at home, and with scepticism, which also came easily to me.

Scientists, among whom I include mathematicians, are often sceptical, or actively hostile about religion. I thought it high time I took some interest in their opinions, and was grateful therefore for the friendships Mary and I formed in Wales not only with Bertrand Russell (see note on Poem 63 and Appendix), but also Professors Patrick Blackett (1897–1974), experimental physicist, whose family had a cottage a couple of miles away, and Joseph Needham (1900–95), biochemist, who often visited North Wales.

Both were Fellows of the Royal Society and pre-eminent among that intellectual galaxy, mostly a long way to the Left in politics, who helped to politicise science during the Thirties and win the war. Needham was the polymath architect, together with his Chinese lady-adjutant, Lu-Gwei Jen (whom he married in old age after his FRS wife's death), of the many-volumed History of Science and Civilisation in China. *Blackett had a Nobel Prize for physics and the Order of Merit. I assumed him to be agnostic. Needham was High Church Anglican, but (apart from foreign decorations) had only been admitted among the Companions of Honour – he called it 'the poor man's OM' – possibly because those who controlled the distribution of awards thought his veneration for Mao Tse-tung excessive in a luminary of the Church of England. Scepticism drew me towards both men. They buttressed my conventional doubts about certain traditional Christian dogmas, and also about the tired routines in which some of the noblest sayings of Jesus, from so many pulpits, for so many years, had been no more than half-breathed into life or invoked to support political campaigns.*

My own spiritual beliefs remain rooted in the two great Commandments stated by Jesus in St Matthew's Gospel – first, to 'love the Lord thy God with all thy heart'; and, second, to 'love thy neighbour as thyself'. I believe therefore in the need and power of love to save the world and in the existence of God; in what shape, I seldom try to imagine, and even less dispute. Why, when, and where, are easier; by faith, too little, and in too few places. Easier too, by contrast with the First Commandment, is the Second. The day I read about it having been proclaimed, in elongated but grand and highly personal form, by someone so independent of all political parties, and so emphatically atheist about the First Commandment as Bertrand Russell, brought me joy. He was speaking in New York just after the war. Just before the war he had been banned from lecturing there and hounded as a sacrilegious libertine. Now he had returned, smothered in honours (OM, Nobel Prize for Literature), to declare himself at Columbia University. The audience was so vast that a second hall had to be wired and queues stretched round the block to hear him. This is what he told them:

> *The root of the matter is a very simple and old-fashioned thing, so simple that I am almost ashamed to mention it, for fear of the derisive smile with which wise cynics will greet my words. The thing I mean – please forgive me for mentioning it – is love, Christian love, or compassion. If you feel this, you have a motive for existence, a guide in action, a reason for courage, an imperative necessity for intellectual honesty. If you feel this, you have all you should need in the way of religion. Although you may not find happiness, you will never know*

the deep despair of those whose life is aimless and void of purpose; for there is always something that you can do to diminish the awful sum of human misery.

This passionate broadside caused such consternation among gatherings of his atheist and agnostic admirers that he had, over and over again, to reiterate that he would have no truck with God and remained as opposed to the Christian Churches as he always had been. (The sentences are omitted from the part headed 'Religion' of a collection of his writings, called Bertrand Russell's Best, *where surely they belong. His praise of Christian compassion gets a casual reference under 'Ethics'.) At our meetings with Bertie and Edith in Wales we never discussed God or religion; not from fear of a row, which would not have happened, but because neither subject arose for long enough. We were talking once of subjects for novels. Bertie suggested remorse. I said that Joseph Conrad had written about remorse, which delighted Bertie, who had found so much in common with Conrad that he had named both his sons after him, but believed that 'nobody reads him now'. When I asked why he had suggested remorse, he answered, 'You know perhaps that much of my life has been spent declaring there is no proof for the existence of God. I should feel great remorse if I came to the conclusion that there is convincing proof.' For the time being I left it at that.*

Jo Needham, on his last visit to us in Wales, left me a pile of his writings, including homilies he had delivered in the chapel of Gonville and Caius College, Cambridge, of which he was Master. In them he takes a God of love almost for granted. His immense erudition, in several tongues, cultures, sciences, and faiths, Eastern and Western, enabled him to cross quite lightly from one to another and seem well suited to the Day of Pentecost, when the Holy Spirit descended on the apostles and they began to speak in a fistful of them.

Patrick Blackett seemed more reserved. He had huge experience in achievement and administration. His earliest big achievement had been to develop the cloud-chamber for the photography of particles, invented by (in his words) 'a shy and enduring genius', Charles Wilson. This enabled me years later to congratulate him on his elevation to Prime Minister Harold Wilson's Upper Chamber, which made him a lord. By 1930 his photographs of cosmic-ray tracks had established the existence of the positive electron. As Director of Operations at the Admiralty during the war he was instrumental in greatly increasing our killing-rate against German U-boats (he had, incidentally, been a midshipman gunnery officer at the Battle of Jutland); and during the Sixties, among much else, turning to the earth's magnetic field, he offered convincing evidence of the theory of continental drift. He once gave me some pages of a tentative autobiography to read. I revised them to make them more human. This did not anger him, but he seemed rather amazed that I had been to such pains. For a time he had advised the Government of India on defence, staying at Viceregal Lodge. He disapproved that I had expected something about the remarkable friendship between the Viceroy's wife Lady Mountbatten and Pandit Nehru. I did not agree; she was part Jewish and very gifted, he the Hindu leader, and their marriage of two minds worth writing about. But he hated publicity. Arrogance, too, he detested. At Glasgow Central Station one public holiday, when a Left-wing grande dame *who had been sailing with us jumped the queue of the ever-patient masses, I thought he had disappeared, and discovered him, profoundly embarrassed, bolt upright and immobile, as if pretending to be a pillar.*

I value three special memories of him. One is his announcement that 'science has been oversold'; the second, after I had misunderstood him as having declared poetry to be 'of little importance', rounding on me in contradiction. Inspiration, he said, of the kind that comes sometimes to poets, or to scientists 'the hunch', had been a launch-pad for many scientific hypotheses of note, later proved to be true. And the third memory is, the morning after his death, reading the account of his tremendous feats in The Times *to Mary during her final illness.*

I should have liked to listen to a discussion between those three about such matters as the Existence of God, Life after Death, and so on. My own role would be, without false humility, that of a child of about twelve, the kind (if they still exist) who asks, 'Mummy, what came before God?' or the Big Bang, or whatever, and 'What is beyond Beyond?' If any or all three answered 'Nothing', I would want to know what will follow after and is beyond Nothing, and what does Nothing look like; with my own answer, that the human mind is not, and (speaking of course of my own) never will be capable of comprehending, let alone answering. As far as things hard to believe go at present, I would stand out firmly, at the very least, for the Resurrection. It arises in connection with certainly two of the poems in my final group.

Three poems remain in the present group:
Poem 83, 'Gracious Speech'. All the poems in this group were written after a period had been well established in the early Sixties known as the New Morality, the Social or Cultural Revolution, or, specifically, the British Discovery of Sex. It meant incidentally the end of innumerable taboos on conversation, language, hair, clothes, and so on, and a general and welcome liberation from intolerant conventions. (I have no poem about a decline from liberation into licence and from scepticism into cynicism.) For me this Speech from the Throne signifies the infinitely sad omission of a poem I tried to write, but could not. It set me thinking about my parents. Theirs seemed a generation cruelly broken into; not just by one but two World Wars, whereas the two generations that came after escaped a Third War, which never happened and stayed Cold. They missed also the new candour that came in after World War Two. 'If only', I wrote in my autobiography, 'it could have happened after, or even before the First, so that they could have shared it with us, their sons and daughters.' Far, far less would have had to be hidden, or suddenly exploded. With openness would have streamed in a giving of love that was always there at heart and, amongst both parents and children, that tactility that is natural to so many now.

Poem 84, 'Love'. On the previous poem I looked back, on this one forward. It has to be related to the friend whose most-favoured poem it has been for some time, to whom this book is dedicated. Here was someone of the future, an experienced peaceful protester, involved with 'the environment', concerned for the safety of our earth and a life also of the spirit, and with two small sons; who, I hope, will inherit from him both.

Poem 85, 'The Gods Are Jealous'. This is the poem many poets must surely have – the one they themselves don't understand. I remember how this one came about. Amabel Williams-Ellis, widow of Sir Clough, and a pioneer of popular science, came to me with a cutting from a scientific journal. It had to do with a famous discovery in the solar system and ended with the phrase 'Farewell, mysterious Jupiter!' 'You're a poet,' she said. 'Make a poem out of that.' Here is the result. I should be sorry to lose it, and leave readers to their own interpretations. Myself, I think it has something to do with innocence.

77
In the Beginning

GENESIS I, 26–7; II, 7, 21–3; V I–2

His hand went to the hollow in his side,
As, held by hers, together they awakened.
She, his lost limb, is throbbing still in him,
As he in her, of all first loves the first,
Formed differently, but alike in innocence,

Wonder, joy, reason, need, and tenderness.
No rivalry, no rift... until the serpent:
'Know your enemies! Learn Competition!',
Whence men as masters, women's wiles, and banners,
And pros, and antis, and correctitudes.

Some in each sex, if likened to the other,
Grow fierce, or furtive. Some, whom Time has failed
Wholly to alienate, acknowledge freely
Subliminal pulsings of shared origin,
When he was robbed, she raised, that night in Eden.

To feel that way...is that to be accursed?
Worlds of some males we've known might be the curse,
And women turn out the same. Happiness might mean
That what's been blest in men returns to women,
And what's been blest in women revives in men.

Eden – that myth. And yet, where could it come from,
To haunt us still, that breath of something lost,
Some broken arc in a sublime equation,
Female and male, one flesh, in God's own image,
Leaving a longing for reintegration?

78
Eurydice

IN MEMORY OF MARY BURN, WHO DIED 10 AUGUST 1974

Begin with enchanted ground
Between the sea and the mountains,
Yellow irises flagging the marsh,
Coronations of gorse by the river,
Back to the waterfall.

Tumbling of white seals
In winter; in summer quicksilver
Under the oaks, with fantails reaching across,

Horizontal almost; almost
Medieval, waiting for angels.

And beneath the groves of oak,
And under the waterfall pool,
Dapple of leaves and stones;
Kaleidoscope.
The path from the road so still.
Then water;
Water suddenly near.

Would not a messenger
            a Messenger
                        a MESSENGER appear?
In Vietnam
        has someone thrown a bomb
            at Archduke Francis Ferdinand,
In Sarajevo
        about manoeuvre time
            a mushroom cloud been seen?
Not yet
        not even illness
            accident held its hand
Magpies in pairs
        red skies at night
            and all that should be green
Time grew
        love deepened
            till that year.

That year he brought her back.
Found her, bewildered,
On the terrible descent,
Shades hurtling past,
Arabs Israelis,

Whoever was fighting then.
That time was given strength
To lead her back,
Hand in hand,
Slowly, painfully.
'You're all I want,' she said
And he could not speak.
Only climb,
Painfully climb,
Back to the light again.

And suddenly he could not bring her back.

Is the truest time the time of greatest strain?

For her the Mozart
Andante. For her, her flowers.
Ash to the waterfall
From the midmost rock;
All order, wildness,
Fearlessly plunging arch,
Like an Olympic dive
Into the torrent's roar.

The sun kneels above Ireland
                    a thin white cloud
                                        bandaged across
Like the head
                    the blindfold head
                                        of someone being beheaded
Earth like the body shudders
                    a few convulsions of light
                                        night's cloak thrown over.

It is All Souls Night.
                    Ask!
                       Does the salesman
The motor-car salesman
                    Arise?
                       Do the genial heathen?
Is there Resurrection
                    For all?
                       Will the hobo
Stiff in a ditch
                    dance at a silver sound?
                       Will Adolf Hitler?
Will the torturers rise again?
                    with those they tortured?
                       the poor?
Will the poor stand up
                    without burdens?
                       the sea?
Will the sea divide?
                    the bleached bones
                       meet and arise?
Will it be possible to reassemble the ashes
Of the football crowds maidens and youths on vases
Sages charioteers Assyrian slaves
And victims of yesterday's news
Crushed in a shriek of steel?
What will become of the Good
Who left bits of themselves to hospitals but said nothing
   concerning
Their souls?... and the Christians?... the golden gates
Will they turn to swing-doors for some, the inner light
Not strong enough to save them from outer darkness?

Will the optimists rise again, the unstable hopers?
Shall I? Will even she,
Whose candle kindles my heart, who seems to have gone

Straight through?
        It is All Souls Night.
                Ask now!
Halloween has gone. The witches are back from the
  moors.
All Saints has gone. The saints have returned to work.
Have we loved enough? Is it right
        [where not applicable delete]
To be [not at all]
            or [slightly]
                or [very afraid indeed]?

The sun returns.
        headlamp, then fireball;
            swelling beyond Manod,
And then in glory over all these hills.
And once she touched my wrist between the sheets,
And something strong as handcuffs gripped the other,
The one time ever I knew Awe.

Touch me again o touch!
        assured of death,
            yet reassured;
As if in her I had known,
        in her did know,
            the element,
Can only do,
        can only give
            one thing,
Give Life,
        called Elixirium;

And once was Orpheus, who brought back Eurydice,
Who leads him now, as he
Follows, with faded coat,

And dobbin Pegasus clip-clop,
Groping his own way to the way that she,
Who was his light, went into light itself

79
A Young Knight's Tomb

IN MEMORY OF A.F.J.

The knights, the knights beside their dames!
I look at this one longest.
Perhaps he was the awkward one,
The not-much-wanted sort of son,
When others rode to tournaments,
Who thought it best to hide.

Perhaps there floated from the tower
The brightest scarf of all.
'Wear it!' she cried; and who can say?
He may have done, but lost the way.
Perhaps his brother took the horse.
Perhaps he could not ride.

Perhaps he died too ill to joust.
Perhaps he loved no woman,
To lie unarmed among the rest
With hands five steeples on his breast,
– So gentle, unforgettable –
And no one at his side.

80

Peace

FOR NICK

A whole half-hour
and you've been reading
I saying nothing
and thinking nothing
unless how quiet I am
how rapt you look
how quiet with your book

a love anthology

Strange that in all those pages
remembering bliss
there is not one
in all those ages
not a single one
half-hour like this

nothing so still
nothing so tranquil

as at this new year you
go south-
ward sunward I
rainward northward
a difference of sky
the view
that was on the left when you came
on the right when I go

Essentially
little is changed there is no
loneliness or not much it is useless
to say
remember it all. You will.
It is pointless to say
thank you since you could only
reply thank *you*
for all those places times.

Everyone knows these lines.

81
Absence

'WHEN YOU ARE OLD AND GREY' ... W. B. YEATS
'QUAND TU SERAS BIEN VIELLE' ...
PIERRE DE RONSARD

When first we met, words tripped on deeds.
Deeds were wild, words disarrayed,
In an impetuous, one-way-street
Collision of immediate needs.

Now lust has cooled, and loving found
More restful, more reflective scenes:
The last a wheatfield, where your hound
(More sprite than hound) kept casual watch

A yard outside our wooded hill;
Or rooms in a deserted house;
A honey-coloured church; a mill;
The time five days from yesterday.

Which, time and place and longing, all
This week of missing you, at night,
I labour at for some remote
Pedantic schoolboy to recite.

It is called work, an anodyne
To cheer the glum insomniac,
Obsessed with mood, half-mad with words,
Whose guts are always two: Come back!

Come here! Come now! And let our words
Revert to their first formless rush!
Be mine! And let the poem go.
For other men the burning bush,

The scalded lips, the Muse's wand,
To make a mill enchanted ground,
And in some Fabergé of a verse
Immortalise your loping hound.

Centuries on, I see a poet,
Deathless laurels round his head,
Handing them back, and begging judges.
'Can I have her, or him, instead?'

Promise of Fame's not worth the cost.
Posterity's the booby's prize,
And no 'That man wrote this for me'
Is worth a cent, once love is lost.

82
Love Continuing

The hamlets sleep beside the watercourse,
Diamond horseshoes shed by a flying horse.
Up in the hills the Bethlehems
Sleep with no problems
Worse than the weather or the price of sheep.
Here, in this Wales too rhythmic to lack sleep,

Awake himself, his second love away,
Sick of the box, tonight's a night to play
Shots, videos of his own, dispense
With lies and violence,
For which all midsummer's had screen enough,
Then go to bed remembering married love.

And there she is, in a boy's arms, their godson,
Laughing towards him, the boy twenty-one,
She seventy, timeless,
A passionate stillness,
To solace or excite. The old takes reappear.
Marriage. Then Europe, in that first freed year,

In '46, to share with him huge hopes,
Safety-net walkers on those smouldering tightropes
Slung between East and West,
Vienna along to Budapest,
Three years in rubble left by the great fire
Between Saint Stefan's crown and Stefan's spire.

And so to Wales, Iron Curtains left behind,
Terror, delations almost out of mind.

'Bliss was it' there to be,
In their own limits, free!
Alive! And home! *'Heureux qui comme Ulysse...'*
Home from the spies, their watched house, the police.

He does not recognise as a torturer,
In her last spool, the death that came to her.
Some pain, no degradation,
But rather a translation
Of the poem she'd made of life; and when she went,
She left him loving as her testament

Against the dark, to do the things they did
With someone else: freeing the grid,
Dipping with rolled-up sleeves
Into the stream to clear the leaves;
Then, God-like, laugh once all the leaves were gone,
Full flowed the stream and all the lights went on.

Fortunate field, that yields a second crop.
Fortunate symphony, that does not stop
When the first movement fails.
Fortunate, fortunate the sails
That shake and swell to so unhoped a breeze,
Back into Life out of Sargasso seas.

Will this time prove illusion by the fall?
Midsummer's dream turn tragicomical?
This change end, must I ask?
As does that play, when all unmask,
Titania as haughty Hippolyta appears,
And Bottom, undeceived, goes off in tears?

O second love, be first continuing
And clasp your hand in mine, that wears her ring.
Such music is without jealousy,

She no Eurydice,
Vanished for ever on a backward glance;
No death; no wraith; a wish, a radiance

Of memory, to which later memory defers,
To merge in a last movement, always hers.
Through joy in both of whom
Age, guilt, misgivings, gloom,
Dissolve, as the Michelangelos begin,
Supine on hills, to paint the morning in.

These thoughts this night have been thanksgiving thoughts,
Deafened and darkened by each day's reports
Of human anguish and disgrace,
But each in its own place
Beyond the storms; and, like a nenuphar,
Safe from the bloodbaths other memories are.

83
Gracious Speech

But oh! The alterations I have seen!
Splendours beyond recall,
With so much else that should have been
Beyond recall
Still on the boards
My Lords.
New rich, new poor,
And some old rich even richer than before.
Sometimes on my walkabouts,
Disguised as I do have to be
To see into the hearts of all my people,
I ask why the old poor go on applauding me,

And how the pensioners manage
To hold their cards above the general scrimmage;
And feel particularly
For certain some
Outwardly keeping olde-tyme equilibrium,
Who stroll compulsively
Among the marvellous young
(The future of my kingdom),
Engaged in unabashed embraces,
And think how hard it was when they were young–
In private, diffidence; rebukes in public places;

Whom, stepping forth from flat,
Bed-sitter and hotel-room, I discover
Wandering in my parks with inbuilt thermostat
To keep a simmering ache from boiling over;
Derided by the sun;
Bodies that half-replied
To other bodies once, the blaze begun
Put out by fear, obedience, or by pride.

These I commend to you.
My Lords and Members of the House of Commons;
And, turning at the door
After my ritual impersonal review
Of national policy and law,
Send my especial messages of sympathy.

For these come no renewings.
Fresh understandings
Of certain private and important things
Have come too late, leaving them high and dry,
To curse in secrecy
Their superannuated rules of right and wrong,
Passing each Saturday what passed them by.
Too old to get, but not too old to long.

84
Love

When flags hang limply from the mast,
Rain comes slanting down,
And every forecast's overcast,
Love still shall wear her crown.

Speech in a loud shop-window age
Sounds shrill beside Love's voice.
Beyond the intellectual rage
Love still shall say 'Rejoice'

To all the lonely, maimed, and plain,
Who long lifelong and long in vain,
Hugging their solitude in pain,
Or hide Despair behind Disdain.

And some who've hungered for a cure,
But could not see one star,
Or tired of search, or weren't quite sure,
Do see, and now they are.

Beyond the orchestras of swords,
Crash and smash and terminal wards,
Frights and fevers, feuds and frauds,
That make our Earth their domicile
To drag the human spirit down,
Love still has shone,
Love still shall smile,
Love still shall wear her crown.

85
The Gods Are Jealous

When I was wandering near my father's house,
There came two lords returning from the chase.
One rode ahead, rode onwards.
I did not see his face.
Power enveloped him, electric. The other lord,
Lovely as I was,

And younger even than I, returned to talk,
Remained to play. At twilight we would play
The first stars out, and once, beside the sea,
He ran a mile away,
And then, with arms outstretched, ran laughing back to me,
Almost into my arms.

Neither had ever known touch, nor ever knew
The touch we then intended.
Frustration always came on the same cue.
Just as we reached to touch, the heavens opened...
Thunder and lightning!...and the deity descended,
The golden rain, the eagle.

We did not seek that grace.
In that bewildered ecstasy each lay writhing,
Eyeballs rolled back, rapt in his wild embrace.
Why chosen, we could not say,
And dared not ask. The ever-jealous god desired us.
Therefore we must obey.

Sometimes he'd come again, in warrior's form.
And when he'd done with us, and set us down,

Guileless once more, by castle or by ocean,
There to resume our games,
Out of a furious sky we heard our names
Called through the thunderstorm

From solitudes that need
Placations past all human things that yearn:
'Danaë, farewell! And farewell, Ganymede!'
And we would answer
'Farewell, mysterious Jupiter!', till his return,
And our capitulation.

GROUP EIGHT

There is a linking of opposites in the poem 'Memorial Meeting' (93) which did not seem to call for any note when first I began to write it. It has to do, on the one hand, with the story of the two disciples ('two dazed bucolics' in the poem), on a journey from Jerusalem to the village of Emmaus, to whom Jesus reveals himself on the morning of his Resurrection, and their intense joy when they grasp what has happened to them; on the other, a woman in an agnostic/atheist sophisticated society, lighting a candle in a dead scientist-husband's memory, furtively, at night, for fear of phoney-commiserating comments ('I'm afraid dear Emma's going religious').

I chanced also to read something that gave me cause to write another note relevant to this final group of poems. In his much-read book The Selfish Gene, *Professor Richard Dawkins praises St Thomas, 'Doubting Thomas', for refusing to believe the other disciples' news that Jesus had risen from the dead until he had seen the evidence, 'in his hands the prints of the nails...and thrust my hand into his side'. Thomas, Dawkins instructs us, demanded evidence, and his story is told not 'so that we shall admire Thomas, but so that we admire the other apostles by comparison, whose faith was so strong they did not need evidence'. It is true that Thomas demanded evidence. The rest of Dawkins's claim is false. The texts, which his students and fans can and should check for themselves, show beyond question that, initially, all the other disciples but one were just as unbelieving as Thomas. The one exception is John with Peter at the empty tomb (John 20. viii). Neither of them saw Jesus, but nonetheless 'that other disciple...believed'. 'That other disciple' means John. Not Peter, who 'went home wondering'. The other disciples are not held up to be admired 'in comparison' with Thomas. Initially all doubted except John, and the women, whom Professor Dawkins does not mention. Thomas himself, after bravely bursting out before they all go to Jerusalem, 'Let us also go, that we may die with him' (John 11. xvi), fled like the others after the arrest of Jesus and is not recorded as following him later to the high priest's house, as did John and Peter. To call him 'the most admirable of the apostles' is fantasy. If doubting is to be the test of reliability, then the whole lot of them were admirable except John, 'the disciple whom Jesus loved', and the women.*

Professor Dawkins was peddling, with cause, and not the first person since Lucretius, the familiar thesis which derides what he calls 'blind faith', upon which religions, and all the damage they do and are doing, often depend. He omits another kind of faith. It is, to my mind, what Patrick Blackett meant by 'the hunch', that sense that comes to someone, man or woman in the street, scientist, artist, poet, composer, doctor, lover, cleric, that they have 'got it right', whatever or whoever it may be, before – even long before – it is actually achieved, even if by somebody else. This is quite different from the vainglory of the dictator set on war, or, in a parliamentary democracy, the self-satisfying sincerity of a president or prime minister. But how easy to confuse the two, and how easy, with a modicum of power, to see to it that in the minds of the mob, or the electorate, they are confused.

I hope few other notes are needed for this last group. Poem 86, 'On the Soul – A Letter To Goronwy Rees', is a lighthearted piece in answer to one of his on television. I saw him in hospital the night before he died; he was then, and had been for some time, in a very different mood, the mood he was in when he wrote me the letter I have quoted in my note on Group Seven. To those readers who, like the seventeen-year-old in my preface, do not know who Pontius Pilate was, Constantine in Poem 94, 'Jesus and the Fig-Tree', is the Roman warrior who was nominated Emperor by the army at York in AD 306 and in 330 made Christianity the official religion of the Roman Empire; his reign thus became the 'right time' for apostles.

In Poem 92, 'The River', Shekinah, in my dictionary, is 'a visible manifestation of the Divine Presence in Hebrew theology'. I have used it as a metaphor in the tale of travellers of whatever faith, who at least have been aware that such a Presence does – or even no more than might – exist, and do not want to lose it.

I regret that the last brief section of Poem 78, 'Eurydice', is not in this final group. All the others seemed just to happen into it. But 'Eurydice' belongs in a long, carefully constructed piece with a set purpose, worked on over many years, and I have left it where it is. Almost all this concluding group relate to Mary's final illness and death and my thoughts afterwards, with one exception, in the sense that I wrote the last poem, 'Thine', more than fifty years ago, and do not think I have changed more than one or two words since. It was said at my father's funeral. I said 'The Lake' at the Mass in London for Mary. I had changed some lines from a poem written and published earlier. The lake is in Cwm Ystradlyn, off the beautiful Cwm Pennant near our home.

86

On the Soul

A LETTER TO GORONWY REES

Dear Accident, or Event (since so I must
Address you, having seen you on the box,
And heard you claim,
Or thought I did, we may not take on trust
Your being as an individual soul),

It seems you're composite of bombarding atoms,
Forever floating in and floating away,
A Bundle of Sensations.
'All is in flux,' Heraclitus used to say.
One can't step in the same Goronwy twice.

Indeed GORONWY, 'stream of crystal water'
In Welsh, becomes you, making you a kind
Of spectral Minnehaha,
And suits your leaping thought and lucid mind,
Dear Fellow of All Souls, who don't exist;

Respected friend, who's really read the books
We think he has; who, quizzed on Diderot,

Burckhardt, de Tocqueville, Hume,
The Commedia, or Choderlos de Laclos,
And especially Goethe, will not change the subject.

I am Sensations too, whom waves and cells
Rush round and through and age inside, and all
Make of this 'I' no more
Than some poor Koestleresque 'grammatical
Fiction', which humbles me, or ought to do.

But since quite early youth, liking to trace
My pedigree through the apes much further back
To fish, amoebae,
And primal slime and fire; sensing a lack
Of thoroughness among most who lectured me

On where we come from, I assumed I owned
(Corrupted, bastardised by countless bars
Sinister) in my veins,
If I may put it so, the blood of stars,
And what made stars, and this I called my soul.

Which then I chose, and choose still to consider
As the beginning of my family tree,
And yours as well;
A form of ancestor-worship, you'll agree,
Possessing poetry, if short on proof;

And hope, when dead...or rather, as you'd say.
When the bombardment stops of what for form
's sake is called Me...
This soul will not be exiled from that swarm
Of life and love; but how, attempt no guess.

An ignorant, vain and sentimental answer
To minds like yours, my dear Goronwy Rees,

If I may steal the tab
Pinned for convenience on your non-existence
By Ministries, the Press, and the Police.

87
In the London Library

He returns the dictionary
Among the shelves marked 'Medical',
And sits for nearly an hour
In a dark corner, frozen,
White in the face.

Here the books live; the people
Have submitted to anaesthesia
To write more books, and his trance,
His cataleptic stare,
Are nothing unusual.

But he is not thinking of Empires,
Prison statistics, the Poor Law,
Ikons, the environment,
Catullus, the bomb, or the Letters
Of Madame de Staël.

But a beautiful woman, wearing
A white maribou jacket,
Who smiles whenever he enters
From pillows, and today is so much
Better, they told him.

For whom a sentence just read
Seems to close her life,

Set it on shelves, and make
The rest of his life a memoir,
An index of her.

Cold seas cover him over;
Till slowly, riding some buoyant
Wave not found in those millions
Of waves of learning, he surfaces
On a thought, a question.

'A disease', the sentence has said,
'That invariably proves fatal.'
A good description of Life.
Rafted on the thought, he goes back.
The question is, How long?

88

Lie at the End

Lie at the end,
Austere and grand,
Who had in life
Such tenderness,

And be for ever
Beyond our fever.
Love will attempt
What Love can do.

So much to ask
That conquering mask,
Still as the moon
Above our town.

Lie there and prove
What might has Love;
If Love can fill
The solitude;

If Love dare cross
The old abyss.
Which, like the world,
Is death, unshared.

89
A Variation on Shakespeare

When other people's verse has sense and metre,
And mine seem squibs, that I believed saltpetre;

When matches splutter, and green logs won't ignite,
Inanimate things transmute into human spite,

Rakes hit me in the face, brooms trap my legs,
Cups smash when looked at, and frying-pans fall off pegs;

When petty losses bring big loss awake,
And holes in pockets tunnel into heartache;

When pots won't boil, and what should rise won't rise,
Then, 'in disgrace with fortune and in men's eyes',

I fold my hands and think of you instead,
And life seems better. And would be, if you weren't dead.

90

The Gospel of Saint Mark

You should do a preambular stint
With Aramaic. You should speak
Hebrew bilingually.
Latin I take for granted, and Greek
(Both Koiné and Septuagint).

A year on the Mishnah makes sense.
The Jews – Hasmonean line,
Economy, topography,
And archaeology round about Palestine.
In relation to both Testaments.

Next, Rome. Make yourself familiar
With the then Empire. Research,
Also, its subsequent policies
And their mark on the quarrelling Church
(Early and later Conciliar).

Contemporary religion
Comes next: Mithra, Osiris, the odd
Mystery (note Eleusinian),
And anything else the pagans groping for God
Built a makeshift bridge on.

Then Higher Criticism (what's still viable).
Don't, if it gets vertiginal,
Take shelter in summaries.
Always read Bultmann in the German original.
The English is unreliable.

You can then start taking a look
At the Gospel itself. The present-day notion
Still puts it first. Never in all
The story of letters have such scholarship, devotion,
Serviced so small a book.

You may then be accepted a true
Christian, and set off to heal
The sick, bring sight to the blind,
Free the poor and imprisoned, and feel
The Spirit of the Lord is upon you.

For the other approach, the short-
Circuit called Faith – I've no right
To recommend or disparage it.
The few good books are old and rather recondite.
I've no idea where it's taught.

91
For Her Letters

Ronsard, Shakespeare, Donne, big-headed lovers,
How can you boast that 'This gives life to thee...'
Or...'what a miracle she was', or *'Ronsard m'aimait...'*.

No one today knows the name of the one you mean.
Your 'immortal verse' has immortalised an Anon.
And if by luck her name, or his, is known,

Their appearance is not. Which might be just as well,
Since a portrait might disappoint. A portrait might show
The kind of person, today, one wouldn't look twice at.

The people to boast are, first of all, the Sumerians,
If it was the Sumerians who invented the alphabet.
If not, whoever enabled her to write letters.

And next J. Nicéphore Niepce and Claude his brother,
And whoever suggested bitumen of Judaea,
Which gave them the fame of having founded photography.

And next myself, in transferred insecurity,
Taking her letters and photographs and burying them
In a bed in the garden at two o'clock in the morning;

And seeing the place by daylight an obvious place
Where someone had buried something, put flowers above;
Then came to my senses and stowed them safe in the bank.

So all young lovers hereafter, in dazzling or dingy
Diamanté or jeans, with your beautiful casual
Leanings towards one another, and your utterly stunning

Impulsive movements of love, if you chance on my words,
And don't believe the superlatives, you can easily check
By asking the bank to surrender you these deposits –

For which I give you carte blanche, well knowing you'll find
My verses Coke to champagne to the one they describe,
As are Ronsard's, Shakespeare's, Donne's, and all the others.

And 'cursed be he' not who 'digs my bones', but who robs
The bank and takes jewels, takes title-deeds,
And scatters anything of hers, thinking it worthless;

To avoid which curse, send me back the originals,
Making copies, thief, for yourself. Hang on to them;
And 'when you are old and grey', in prison or out,

In your penthouse apartment, '*auprès de la chandelle*',
Take down those copies; study them; make up your mind
If you ever nicked anything, deed or jewel, their equal.

92

The River

After long underground the river surfaced. Gleaming
Like sword-blades burnished, it became horizons,
As well as visions glimpsed an age ago, and brought
To certain travellers fresh and sad perceivings
How parched their lives were now;

How clear clean waters,
Whether bright crystal falls from high in the hills
Leached into by farm and factory,
Or stately deltas
With ports-of-call where oil changed into gold, then gold
To blood, were cursed,
Not just as carriers of sickness,
But worse, far worse, becoming Heart-of-Darkness rivers,
Polluters of men's souls...
All, except this one,
That, plunging to stay pure,
Had gone from sight; or almost.

Sometimes some travellers might stumble on it.
Or was it the river curving to meet them?
As if an elemental force could be aware
Of mortals needing it and, when it plunged,
Made sure they knew where to hew. Jungles could not
expunge

That sense of where it flowed, and on its banks
Would be familiar jetties, remembered pools, and inns
Where children danced, and tigers stalked to drink,
Sheep wandered to be dipped, and lovers slept in peace.

The travellers were not of the hysterical
Prophetic category, whose hair turns white
At a sudden shock, or across whose breasts
Lightning might leave indelibly a pattern,
That could be off their pullovers, or their blouses,
Peculiar to them; or a forgotten language,
Waiting to be decoded. They behaved the way
Each of them had behaved the days before the day
The river surfaced; buttoned their ecstasy-
Proof waistcoats, sprayed themselves
With anti-revelation aerosol,
And stepped out firmly with rose-demisted spectacles
Back to the humdrum;
But never willingly
Left out of mind the river.

Even a night without it troubled them.
Some feared they'd sicken, many probably would
Go berserk if it disappeared for good.
They said it could not, but could not say why.
Simply it seemed, since first they gazed in one another,
The river could no more lose their reflection
Than they the river from their inmost eye.

Time, blearing the best of days, save that day.
River, Shekinah river, stay with them. Stay.

93
Memorial Meeting

After the basketsful of letters answered, she takes her place
In the familiar Hall, his colleagues round her,
Hands folded, almost royal…
                                        Eczema
Of the paranormal! Of all times
To come on now, that infantile complaint!

The orations start. Comparisons with Newton,
Tributes from Africa… And once again
That allergy, brought on by
'A natural Christian. We shall pray for him',
A priest's outrageous misappropriation.
At such a moment, to have brought up *that*.
In such an audience.

Schubert begins. His students asked for Schubert:
Music, the always allied discipline.
And there they are, the young, the grave, the eager
Faces that hung on his; and the notes, as they spin
Their exquisite compelled dance,
Change to the symbols of a dead scientist
Moving so elegantly along the page,
Someone once said, 'They should be keyed and played.'

Now 'Fear no more', the dirge from *Cymbeline*;
All wanted that, the humanists' St Paul.
At 'Home art gone', a pricking behind her eyes
Remembering homes, and rooms, and many travels,
Till 'Fear not slander'. Slandered, fearless he!
From earliest days, his first laboratory,

Where anything might be proved, except by wishing it,
The only sin. She looks that way. She sees
A Chinese screen of leaves, beyond the leaves
Obvious, infinite, and blue Unknown,
Dwarfing all genius. How well he knew it...
Newton's last words. How like a Stoic shed
His own, excellence by excellence,
Sure that his work would grow, others improve on it...

And once again that itch. O infinity
Of love, of loneliness!
Could it come from a blind spot? Were he and she
So adamant for evidence, so passionately
Pure in their dispassion they fell victims
To passion not to wish, itself a wish?

Rising composed, she thanks the Chancellor,
Greets former students, friends, the foreign delegates,
And joins the family. 'It went well...the Government
Were represented, after all...*Cymbeline* was just right.'
And the chairs begin to be piled.

Somewhere quite other
Two dazed bucolics walk a country road,
Beside them someone they have failed to recognise,
Till they too start to itch.
Next morning, in College Chapel,
Doors clang on empty aisles, where an unexpected
Candle, placed there, it must have been in secret,
Still burns; burns down, staining the yellow stone.

94
Jesus and the Fig-Tree

Figs were not in season.
On the face of it, a poor reason
For Jesus to get so angry.
Perhaps he was hungry.

I think, when he put a curse on
The fig-tree, he was cursing the person
Who says, 'It isn't the moment.'
It never is the moment.

How did Jesus manage to stop
Shrivelling things up?
After all those healings,
What a relief to his feelings

To curse, if only a tree!
The apostles were sure to flee.
But he never cursed them.
Oh no, he rehearsed them

For a really difficult time
(The good times came with Constantine)
And they answered his call,
When it wasn't the moment at all.

They didn't shrivel.
To my mind a lot of drivel
Comes from critics who get in a dig
At Jesus cursing the fig.

95
The Lake

I've often dreamed that someone else
Will one day feel the way I've felt
And say so after I am dead
In words or phrases I once made;
And now and then I've tried to guess
Which words they'd be, and what the cause.
But when at last the moment came
It had not been in any dream.

In a green collar-bone of hills,
A stone's-throw from the sky, in Wales,
We came upon a little tarn,
So sky-reflecting, taciturn,
So white, expectant, and enchanted –
An air-strip for a magic carpet –
It seemed that all the western myths
Had risen from its peaty depths.
Three boat-lengths thick all round the shore
The water-lilies were in flower,
And kingcups thrust their yellow heads
Between the blue glass of the reeds.
And looking at that lake I felt
A century or two annulled.
And other men would one day be
Exactly as I was that day,
With her beside me then, and living,
Beside me still, though lost, still loving,
Still lovely, still beloved, still giving.
The longing tugging at my heart
Had tugged at people in the past,

And would at many unborn people:
To utter thanks, and be unable.

96
Open Day and Night

I ask so sadly,
As one not prone to sadness,
Can all these words,
That you believed would be written
Be written, go on being written,
And you not read them?

Won't you come back,
Through whom I came to write them?
Since, without you,
I should have stayed all mind,
The words in my heart would have perished
With none to feed them.

Loveliest of all
(Say it I may, since all said it),
I cork them, seal them
Into bottles and throw them at midnight
On rivers the stars divide.
Somehow, receive them.

Sweetheart, my only
Love, if love means lifetime,
Transmit, as always,
So lightly, your great answers.
This position's open all day;
And at night, to dream them.

97
The Other One

I have observed how men react to pain
When the inquisitors get down to work:
How some give everything away at once,
Some guard a little for a little time,
And some gasp out a memorable phrase
That might come from a last speech in the dock,
Or on the scaffold, when such things were granted.
And some like me, foul-mouthed, ignorant,
Cursing relieves, it doesn't matter what...
Spit, curse, revile, the nearest within reach;
Thereby, as now I know, but did not then,
Missing the greatest chance in history
Of instant Paradise, unlike my mate.

I am the thief on the forgotten cross,
The one they crucified, who railed on Christ.
Among whatever stars your Kingdom be,
I beg you, Lord, though late, remember me.

98
Thine

Thine was the chaos; Thine was the creating.
Thine was the clay alone, and Thine the mating.
Thine was the innocence, and the unfolding.
Thine the intransigence, and Thine the moulding.

Thine is the web, and Thine is the unweaving.
Thine disbelief, and Thine the green believing.
Thine ages' toil, and Thine a day's undoing.
Thine has been ruin; Thine is the renewing.

Thine is the intellect, and Thine the feeling.
Thine the withholding; Thine is the revealing.
Thine is the falling-off, Thine the repenting.
Thine was the sentence; Thine is the relenting.

Thine is the trust, and Thine is the despairing.
Thine the wild wreck, and Thine the onward-faring.
Thine the indifference, and Thine the striving.
Thine is the death, and Thine is the surviving.

Appendix

FOR EDITH RUSSELL

At the beginning of his biography of Bertrand Russell, volume two, published in 2000, after the title page and dedication, Ray Monk has placed two epigraphs:

> 'The greatness of a man is to be measured by his intelligence minus his vanity.'
>
> Attributed to Prince Otto von Bismarck
>
> 'Madness alone is truly terrifying.'
>
> Joseph Conrad, *The Secret Agent*

On the first page of his preface to volume two Monk writes:

> Russell's life seems to have been inextricably drawn towards disaster, determined on its course by two fundamental traits of character: a deep-seated fear of madness and a quite colossal vanity.

And in the preface to his second volume:

> [Russell] was, it sometimes seems, simply not capable of loving another human being... He could imagine – and frequently did imagine – extending the boundaries of his own ego, but what he could not imagine was reaching out *beyond* them. Would that this were only a theoretical problem, but the experience of Russell's wives, children and friends suggests that, on this point, theory and practice combined in the most devastating manner.

The intended reference to Bertrand Russell of those two remarks attributed to Bismarck and Joseph Conrad are obvious, and I must take issue with them; as also with the direct comment on him immediately above by Professor Monk. Bertie died in 1970. Edith Finch was the fourth of those wives Monk mentions, and Mary and I among those friends who knew him well during, at least, the last decade of his eighteen years of marriage to her. Mary died in 1974. Edith wrote me a most loving and wise letter about her and I sent her my Poem 63 in shared bereavement. She lived on until 1978, unhappily into the initial stages of what became a widespread debunking of him. I begged her, for future historians, to write down her own versions of facts, her own ripostes, and once, as early as February 1971, she replied:

> I should be infinitely happy to be able to contribute something to a just understanding of him. If I seem to work myself into a fuss, even to the point of incoherence, it is because of the desperate sense of my own inadequacies and the desolating frustration of finding no words to express what I know to be true – frustration not lessened by the knowledge that the impact and credibility of whatever I say, that is contrary to what my interlocutor thinks, or suspects, or wishes to think, is lessened in his mind by the fact that I love Bertie entirely.

'Entirely' is the word which Bertie, in chapter two, volume three of his autobiography, uses of their enchanted honeymoons across Europe and Britain; and, in summarising the enchantment, adds:

> We found that we not only loved one another entirely, but the satisfaction we found grows seemingly without limit into an abiding and secure happiness and is the basis of our lives.

Is there anything more to be said? Yes, because, whatever Bertie (and Edith) may say, 'it sometimes seems' to Professor Monk that Bertie was 'simply not capable of loving another human being'. This may have some explanation in the character of Professor Monk, and indeed in the introduction to his first volume he grants that the personality (of Russell) he has revealed in his two volumes 'is one that many will find repellent, but it has not been my aim to present him in an unfavourable light'. But something has upset him. I as a reader am uncomfortably aware that, page by page, he dislikes Russell more and more. This has to do with that dread of madness which he senses in Russell and Russell's consequent attitude to his son John. It also helps to explain the space Monk gives to the suicide by self-conflagration of Russell's granddaughter Lucy, the most horrifying among a cluster of family insanities; of which, had Ibsen put them on the stage, his most fervent admirers might have said that he had gone too far. They form the long finale to Monk's second volume, entitled *The Ghost of Madness*. I do not think them the right way to end a biography of Bertie.

The answer, to my mind, why they are there is, to use a frequently mocked-at phrase of his, a very simple one. It lies in the omission by Monk of something in a poem by Bertie. The poem, to be found on a title page of the first volume of his autobiography, has the dedication 'To Edith' and two verses. Monk quotes the first verse in his brief introduction to his own first volume, entitled *The Spirit of Solitude*. Here it is.

> Through the long years
>   I sought peace.
> I found ecstasy, I found anguish,
>   I found madness,
> I found loneliness.
>   I found the solitary pain
> That gnaws the heart,
>   But peace I did not find.

The second verse does not follow. I assumed Monk must be keeping it for his second volume. I ransacked both volumes, but it was not there. This amazed me. Here it is, from the autobiography, meant for Edith, immediately after the first verse, where it should be:

> Now, old & near my end,
>   I have known you,
> And, knowing you,
> I have found both ecstasy & peace,
>   I know rest.
> After so many lonely years,
> I know what life & love may be
> Now, if I sleep,
> I shall sleep fulfilled.

'Madness' is out. 'Loneliness' is out. Edith had driven them out, but his biographer, for some reason, has omitted their expulsion. Within two years of their marriage she had given him the assurance to compose and deliver that broadcast so widely heard and held in memory called 'Man's Peril', 'Remember your humanity and ... the way lies open to a new Paradise.' 'Anguish' is still in the poem; she told me of the anguish on his face watching as his elder son John was taken away to hospital, an event almost coinciding with that broadcast. 'Ecstasy' is there because he had insisted that it should be...and, she added, laughing, 'I know people suppose us past it, and you are curious. But I shall not give you chapter and verse.' In fact I knew already from someone who happened to be attending both Russells at night and should not have told me. Edith should have had a memoir to herself, or a chapter in some book about women married to men of genius, and what they meant to them. She saved Bertie from madness, or despair like madness, I am sure of that, remembering the ones in that family who inherited or brought madness into it from outside, and found nobody free enough to help them. (How can I forget them...one of them so tragically like my own sister Stella?) Edith and Bertie did their best for the children and grandchildren, over many years, but also had, as it seems to me, their own new, destined life to lead, beginning when he was eighty and she fifty-one and not expecting to have to be a grandmother.

I cannot imagine any future biography of him ending without her as central, and should like it to include two memories of mine. One is, she told me how she fell in love. It happened at Oxford, in the Cadena Café in the Cornmarket, in about 1920, when she would have been nineteen. She was studying at St Hilda's, completing her American education begun at Bryn Mawr Women's College, Philadelphia. She fell not at first sight, but on first hearing. She heard someone laughing so infectiously, she had to know who it was, and was told 'Bertrand Russell', then not quite fifty. Years later, married to the laughter, she described it as of the rolling kind that 'makes other people laugh even when they don't know what they're laughing about'.

The other story comes from the time when she was dying. I had left her at Bangor Hospital with Conrad Russell and gone back to the house, Plas Penrhyn, where she and Bertie had lived and planned and plotted and the grandchildren spent their childhood. I had passed the night there in the room next to the bedroom she and Bertie shared. She would not afford a nurse, and I was scared she might sleepwalk into the (one-bar) electric fire. I collected whatever I had left behind and, out of curiosity, looked inside the bedroom A painting hung above the double-bed. A painting of a dove. I thought, I've seen that dove before. But it was not Picasso's dove. It was a copy of the dove in Piero della Francesca's painting of the Baptism of Christ. And I thought, how strange, above her and Bertie, those two, considered to be unbelievers. On second thoughts, it seemed not strange at all. At the time of his debate with the Jesuit Father Copleston in 1948 Bertie had told him that, when he wanted to shock people, he called himself an atheist; when he did not, he called himself agnostic. At the beginning of the extremely serious and dignified debate itself he stated: 'My position is agnostic.' In my obituary of Edith in *The Times* I wrote: 'Like him, an agnostic with a religious temperament, she believed as ardently as he did in mankind's need for a spiritual life.'